GIANLUCA SPOSITO

RULES FOR THE PERFECT SPEECH

TOOLS AND SUGGESTIONS FOR EFFECTIVE COMMUNICATION

intra

Rhetorically Series

www.intrapublishing.com
info@intra.pro

ISBN 979-12-5991-497-2

INDEX

INTRODUCTION

To make a good speech there is no precise recipe: the only requirement is to have a set of quality products to draw on to create, from time to time, a unique dish.

The speaker is like the *chef* in the kitchen, who creates from raw materials. But they should know them, they should know the chemical and physical qualities of each element, they should know everything that can happen by combining different elements; they should experiment, try, practice.

Similarly, the orator also creates, over the years, their own pantry made up of readings, study and commitment. And it is only through this progressive building of knowledge and exercise that they will be able to address any kind of oratorical need.

The true orator is not one who is blessed by nature with a smooth and charming eloquence, and without an adequate "pantry" one will soon notice that their *menu* is repetitive and common. Even if they are able to get away with it in some limited occasions (as long as they are similar), they will show all their limits in contexts that are just slightly different or if solicited by more technical and skilled speakers.

On the other hand, the variables are infinite: I certainly can't manage a speech at a condo meeting and an inaugural speech at the White House in the same way; just as I can't make use of a given metaphor in different contexts, repeating it to the point of exhaustion just because in one case it seems to have worked.

However, if my pantry is full of products that I know in depth, it will be easy to understand what I can use and how to use them to make a unique 'dish', which will be memorable each time: not because it should necessarily go down in history, but only (and this is no small thing) so that it can reach my interlocutors and remain fixed in their memory, perhaps even guide their choices.

Today, in order to be effective, communication should be based on a balanced mix of primary elements such as rhetoric, psychology, non-verbal and paraverbal communication. But – be careful – it should be 'superior quality elements' and not collected on the web or through some self-styled *guru*, only able to suggest tips and tricks that – according to him or her – should make you into the best speaker in the world.

Those who are about to read this book should abandon such dreams of glory: I certainly won't be the one to make you into what only you can become. But I would like to accompany you along a path made up of indications (the 'rules', in fact) on how to form and use what I can consider a necessary 'pantry': so that you always have what you need to be able to excel. The quantities, then, will vary as needed, and only the sensitivity and the competence matured will allow to make the "add to taste" (q.s. – *quantum satis*) a concept not approximate but an indication that can be applied naturally.

In short, the realistic objective of this manual is to make the reader aware of the many facets of the art of oratory, of the enormous wealth of knowledge and constant commitment that are necessary for it to be practiced correctly and effectively. It is certainly a manual against improvisation lacking in values, but it is also a manual in favor of the valorization of personal abilities and aptitudes that can only be validly exploited and amplified with adequate study and constant exercise.

More than a set of rules, I would then speak of a multidisciplinary approach to the perfect “speech”. Did I then perhaps get the title of the book wrong?

THE BASICS OF THE ART OF ORATORY

The art of saying

Every day, each of us makes an untold number of speeches, for a variety of purposes: from the early morning email to our supervisor or employees, to the report given during a face-to-face or videoconference meeting, to the argument in court, to the marriage request to our loved one. And there is no denying that in all of these cases, there is always the need to be effective, achieving the intended goal.

What is less known is that – in all the cases listed and in many more – there is an unconscious use of rhetoric. Rhetoric is everywhere, yet few people know what it really is and where exactly it manifests itself. Many think they have caught a glimpse of it in the speech of an incompetent politician, or a long-winded and inconclusive office manager. And yet, this is not it: because rhetoric has nothing to do with these examples of ugly contemporary communication. On the contrary: it is not present in them.

The adjective "rhetorical" today identifies what is

redundant, pompous, useless: a "rhetorical" speech would be, therefore, a speech that aims at the effect and not the substance, where the glitter of the form tries to embellish the emptiness or, better, to distract and lead away the reader or listener from that. One is defined 'rhetorical' when has nothing particular to say but tries to say it with special effects.

The adjective 'rhetorical' can end up labelling the speaker as dishonest, who has made a profession out of the use of that 'emptiness', bamboozling and seducing others, often for questionable purposes (from swindlers to politicians, to dictators).

The passage of rhetoric from science to 'meretriciousness' was therefore the last mile traveled by what, however, is and remains a noble art that we all use daily, without knowing and without necessarily evil purposes.

In fact, our written and spoken language is full of rhetorical figures and patterns, mostly unconsciously (but often incorrectly) realized. From when we wake up and, looking out at the pouring rain, we console ourselves with the rhetorical figure of irony ("What a beautiful day!"), to when we bump into and blame the "table leg" at breakfast using a catachresis, to when we don't go to sleep because we're "dead tired" using yet another hyperbole.

But there's more: even when we think about what to say to someone, how to expound a concept, how to try to get them to accept our thesis, we use elements that rhetoric has long identified and proposed as points of reference for the speaker of every context and time. Yes, because knowing and knowing how to use rhetoric allows one to organize one's own thought into a well-founded and persuasive discourse (a persuasion not by seduction but based on rational argumentation).

Therefore, **rhetoric** is and should remain the art of saying, that is, of speaking and writing in an effective and persuasive way, used by the ancient Greeks and Romans and then transmitted to later cultures; an art that makes use of certain expressions and constructs, called rhetorical figures. Historically, rhetoric is the art intended to allow the speaker to communicate; to make their presence felt to effectively reach the listener (or reader) and lead them to agree with their thesis.

The development of rhetoric is intertwined with that of philosophy, especially Greek philosophy. Aristotle considered rhetoric the opposite of logic: logic seeks the truth, rhetoric the plausible.

After all, it is well known: truth belongs exclusively to the logical-mathematical sciences. In all human sciences, from law to ethics, one cannot argue on rational grounds in the same way as in mathematics or logic. On the contrary, one can demonstrate resorting also to persuasion, therefore to strategies of a rhetorical nature. Persuasion, on the other hand, is also open to the irrational and the emotions that prevail in human relationships.

Rhetoric is then an art. But the term is ambiguous, it defines a simple technique as well as the genius of the creator. Yet, even the genius will eventually make use of the same artifices, intellectual or emotional, that rhetoric can teach. And so the "best speaker" is an "artist", in the sense that they are capable of finding arguments that are as effective as they are unexpected, and of using (rhetorical) figures that no one had thought of, and which are more effective.

The **orator** is therefore the one who 'speaks' (both orally and in writing) to an audience (of listeners or readers): from the lawyer during a closing argument, to the manager during a meeting, to the writer in a book. **Oratory** is therefore the art and technique of public speaking in a persuasive way, to obtain – through the use of different tools – the consent of the audience.

Eloquence – another term that is often used – is the art of expounding arguments in an appropriate, elegant and persuasive manner. In essence, it is the product of rhetoric: the eloquent speaker is the one who, using the art of rhetoric, is able to build an argumentatively sound speech and convey it effectively, persuading those who read or listen.

Different, instead, is the concept of **dialectics**. In the philosophical language the term 'dialectic' has had different meanings, according to the time and the single thinkers. With extreme simplification, it can be argued that dialectics – unlike rhetoric – has as its purpose the demonstration and not the persuasion, realized through short questions and answers (method used, for example, by Socrates in contrast to the long speeches of the Sophists who were the forerunners of rhetoricians).

In a much more general (and non-technical) sense, dialectics identifies the art of dialogue, of arguing, as the technique and skill of presenting the right arguments to prove a point, to persuade an interlocutor, to make one's point of view triumph over that of the antagonist.

Truth does not exist

Unlike logic (think of mathematics), rhetoric does not admit and does not seek the truth, but the plausible. Besides, it is quite obvious: in all human disciplines, from law to ethics, one cannot argue on rational grounds as in mathematics or logic. On the contrary, one can demonstrate resorting also to persuasion – and, therefore, to strategies of a rhetorical nature.

Mathematics shows us that "2+2" makes "4", without any space to argue otherwise; so much so that this logical-mathematical demonstration can be done even by a robot. Vice versa, rhetoric can profitably operate in all the fields in which it is possible to say and contradict; and at the moment the human work is not replaceable. Let's think about law: the truth that is reached at the end of a trial is certainly not comparable to the truth of the logical-mathematical disciplines: it is only a relative truth, a truth called 'procedural', reached through argumentation and reasoning and operating always and only in the field of what is 'probable'.

In these fields the speaker does not "demonstrate", but "argues". Each orator, in the end, will only be able to limit themselves to propose something plausible, credible and acceptable. And possibly with a degree of plausibility, credibility and acceptability higher than that of their (possible) opponents.

This is true as much for a lawyer as for a judge: the search for truth can only be an aspiration, because – in fact – any conclusion can never equal the absoluteness of logical-mathematical truth. More than one, single and absolute truth, we could therefore speak of several 'truths'.

Persuasion and persuasive speech

The speaker, more or less eloquent, should make plausible and persuasive speeches. But what is a speech?

A **speech** is any verbal production (written or oral), consisting of one or more sentences, with a certain unity of meaning. However, beware: rhetoric does not apply to all speeches, but only to those that aim to persuade. For example, a prayer is a speech, but it is certainly not aimed at persuading, just as a sentence is not. Whereas a defense plea and an advertising slogan are.

Rhetoric is based, then, on persuasive speech. Similarly to rhetoric, **persuasion** has long had a bad (and undeserved) reputation. This is because there is a tendency to identify the only possible form of persuasion in the one that seduces without arguing, even ending up putting on the same level persuasion, fiction and lies. To persuade means to induce someone to believe something, sure. But it is not in itself a negative concept (in the sense implying 'manipulation'), as long as the premises from which one starts are not false and there is logical correctness in reaching conclusions (always questionable). Otherwise, we fall into the different (and harmful) area of persuasion by seduction.

Rhetorical persuasive discourse is achieved by making use of rational and emotional instruments. The first are represented by the **arguments** that you choose for your speech (we are in the field of reasoning, the Aristotelian *lògos*), while the emotional instruments are the *pàthos* (the set of passions to raise in the audience) and *èthos* (the personality of the speaker, but also their overall credibility).

The **argumentation** can therefore be defined as a set of demonstrations, even independent of each other, but converging towards the same conclusion, which can be reached by mastering and skillfully mixing the rational and emotional elements, according to classical rhetoric.

However, the rules for a 'good argumentation' are different from those for a 'good demonstration'. For example, a good argumentation should be persuasive, in that it should convince the interlocutor, while a good demonstration should be true (or plausible) and relevant even if not necessarily persuasive. To understand this difference one can think of television talk shows: between a good demonstration and a bad argumentation, the latter wins only for its persuasiveness. A persuasive argumentation can convince even if it breaks the law of logic by starting from false or irrelevant premises with respect to the thesis to be represented. Persuasiveness is therefore very dangerous and, often, fallacious reasoning passes for good. In summary: it makes even a deceit appear sensible.

The audience

The speaker, since ancient times, has always had an 'audience'. Communication sciences defines it as the recipient. What is certain is that, regardless of its name, it has always played a fundamental role, because it has inevitably oriented the choices and behaviors of any speaker.

Already the Pythagoreans distinguished arguments and speeches according to the type of audience: to them we owe the first theory of *kairós* ('opportune'), a concept understood as numerical harmony and closely related to *polytropía*, which instead indicates the degree of appropriateness of a speech in relation to the audience that is in front.

The audience is basically the set of those to whom the speaker addresses their argument: it is a definition that includes a single interlocutor, as well as a large assembly, or even a larger group, and makes no difference between written or oral productions, or – as a borderline case – the inner speech with itself (where speaker and listener coincide).

The first necessary step that any speaker, at any time and in any circumstance, should take is precisely that of "knowing" the audience they are addressing. This is not an easy task, especially when you are not dealing with a dialogue situation (in presence), or when there is an audience that is not visible and even less knowable (think of a television or web audience). This is because in a face-to-face dialogue, the speaker can easily modulate and adjust their speech according to the reactions of the audience (the responses received, body expressions, etc.), while in a situation with an audience not physically present, the speaker will have fewer parameters of reference, especially to adjust their speech or dialogue.

Just as in a written speech, the speaker can (and should) only 'imagine' the audience, adapting all choices in advance.

From now on, having necessarily clarified this definition, we will continue by not distinguishing – where not necessary – between written and oral discourse, and thus speaking generically of 'audience'.

CONSTRUCTING A SPEECH

The parts of persuasive speech

The traditional organization of rhetorical discourse into five parts, corresponding to the same number of skills required of the orator, is absolutely current: *inventio* (research of arguments), *dispositio* (organization of arguments), *elocutio* (way of expressing oneself), *memoria* (memorization), *actio* or *pronuntiatio* (way of delivering). While the first three were linked to both written and oral speeches, the last two (*memoria* and *actio*) pertained exclusively to oral speeches. The *memoria* concerned the memorization of the speech; the *actio* or *pronuntiatio* consisted in the actual declamation and recitation (voice modulation, gestures, posture).

The *inventio* is fundamental in the construction of the discourse, because it is that part of rhetorical science that offers the tools to search and find the arguments on which to build precisely a discourse (arguments that will then be expressed through the *elocutio*). It uses a specific partition: *exordium* (exordium), *narratio* (narration of the facts), *demonstratio* (argumentation of one's thesis), *peroratio* (peroration or epilogue).

The exordium

The aim of the exordium was, for classical rhetoric, to make the audience (the judge and the jurors, but also the public) benevolent, attentive and flexible. Among the various types of beginnings, we recall the affectation of modesty or declaration of inadequacy (consisting in confessing one's own inadequacy and considered an effective tool in that it tends to raise a natural motion of sympathy towards those in difficulty), the declaration of brevity (exemplified by the "I will be brief" of many speeches, even modern ones), the visibly artificial "I remind myself", and the clarification of the motivations that prompted the speaker to write or talk.

These are often simulated forms of humility (of *understatement*, we might even say) that also include the "**plural of modesty**" (*pluralis modestiae*) or the impersonal (*it is said, it is supported*), or other formulas always tending to replace the first person (*the writer, the speaker, the author of these notes,* etc.).

A particular type of exordium is the **insinuation** (so called insinuation exordium). It consists in dissimulating the thesis that is being argued, in going along with the presumed resistance of the audience, pretending to share their opinions or even prejudices, and then winning their trust. It requires a true and proper "insinuation" into the soul of the audience, in order to gain compassion, a "credit", which cannot be explicitly asked for: *"I come to bury Caesar, not to praise him"* (Shakespeare, *Julius Caesar*).

The narratio

The narratio or narration is the telling of facts. It is a true, or rather, plausible story because – we should remember – rhetoric is not a mathematical science (where, instead, the "truth", the "two plus two equals four" prevails). As we have already pointed out, the orator operates in the field of *dóxa* (opinion), not of *alétheia* (truth): they use in their argument the enthymeme, i.e., a form of syllogism that argues from premises that are not absolutely certain but plausible, and produces a conclusion that is equally not certain but plausible. Moreover, a mediocre speaker can make even objectively true facts seem scarcely credible; while a good speaker can give credibility even to facts that are only plausible. But any speech should also include a persuasive narrative.

Of the three ways in which rhetorical persuasion is implemented (*docēre*, to inform; *commovēre,* to move; *delectare*, to please), fundamental and characteristic for the narration of facts is informing. However, in order to achieve its purpose, the narration should also please, that is, make itself heard and not bore. In the *narratio,* one can choose between an *ordo naturalis* (natural order – following a precise chronological order) and an *ordo artificialis (*artificial order – linking the facts in an artificial way that is not tied exclusively to temporal data). For example, in this second hypothesis, one can choose to introduce in the story some discordances (anachronism) between the order in which the events to be narrated happened and the order in which they are narrated. Therefore, it is possible to begin *in medias res* (with the action already started) and then narrate by analepses (or by flashback) the preceding facts; or anticipate by prolepses (or flashforward) subsequent events that will then be resumed and detailed. The evident characteristic of the *ordo artificialis* is that of breaking down the temporal linearity and dividing it into mobile sequences – doesn't this remind you of the way many television dramas of recent years are narrated?

Whatever the choice, the *narratio* should still possess three qualities and be: *brevis* (short – *brevitas*), *perspicua* (clear) and *verisimilis* (plausible).

Classical rhetoric offers an interesting, modern and still usable tool for verifying the conditions necessary for the completeness of the *narratio*. This is a specific scheme consisting of a grid of questions (so-called **topical**, or set of ***loci*** or **common places**) that in fact represent the 'circumstances' to be considered in the exposition of the facts and therefore in the construction of the speech:

quis?	Who?
quid?	What?
cur?	Why?
ubi?	Where?
when?	When?
quomodo?	How?
quibus auxiliis?	By what means?

It is a grid of 'empty' forms (topical grid, that is, of common places – from the Greek *tópos*, 'place'), to be filled with the facts to be narrated.

This grid recalls the "5 W rule" of Anglo-Saxon journalism, given to aspiring journalists and a basic tool to be applied (by answering the grid of questions) for the realization of a news piece (speech):

who? – what? – why? – where? – when?

Cicero also suggests to insert, in the representation of facts, a more immediate representation of reality. The tool to do so is the *evidentia* (living description or representation). This is a figure that allows you to represent the facts "putting them almost before the eyes of the listeners," so that they can directly live the evidence and emotional effectiveness of this sensory experience.

Precisely because of these characteristics, *evidentia* is also a very effective stylistic device for obtaining an effect of plausibility and it can be compared to images (a subject studied in visual rhetoric). For this reason, *evidentia* is something more than simple clarity, because clarity concerns only the comprehensibility of the text, while *evidentia* indicates its sensory fruition (therefore additional to clarity itself), so that facts are not simply exposed, but directly shown. Thus, through *evidentia*, the maximum persuasive power of the image is achieved: it is the image (of facts) painted in words.

All of the above is used, nowadays, under the much more exotic name of storytelling.

Storytelling

Although storytelling merely mixes up and names things already seen since the era of classical rhetoric, passing through centuries of artistic-literary tradition, here we analyze its main patterns.

Monomyth or also called the hero's journey: many modern stories follow the Ulysses model, from Star Wars to Walt Disney stories. The hero, having decided to embark on a new life, returns home with a reward or enriched with new wisdom, something that will help themselves and their group to which they belong.

The Mountain: it is the narrative representation of a *climax* (a rhetorical figure that – we will later see – is also called gradation and can be ascending or descending). Its structure is realized so that the tension or the drama are held up with a constant climb towards the climax, a fundamental moment of the narrative story; and also through an emotional up and down to hold the interest of those who read or see and listen (think, once again, to the seriality of the most recent tv series).

Nested loops, or 'concentric circles': these are several narrative structures that intersect with each other. The narrative containing the main message or story interacts with others that are intended to fulfill or clarify it.

Sparklines, or 'bright lines': this is a narrative structure in which the discourse unfolds on two opposing plans that are continually intertwined. They compare what is with what could be. It is considered a highly emotional technique and therefore engaging.

In medias res, that is, with the action already underway: this is exactly the scheme of the *exordium* proposed by classical rhetoric, consisting precisely in starting one's own story from its decisive moment. Therefore, the interest of the audience is kept high and the audience, intrigued, is then guided to the discovery of what were the dynamics that led the protagonist to that precise moment.

Converging Ideas: it consists of a discursive structure in which different strands of thought converge to form a single idea. It can be used to show how an idea is the result of several minds or elements that have contributed to its evolution.

False Start: the narrative begins with a seemingly predictable plot that is abruptly interrupted to give way to a change of course, which will lead to a new beginning. This format is considered particularly suitable to talk about a moment in which you had to face a failure, then overcome it by reaching new goals.

Petal Structure: this scheme is an ideal discursive structure for organizing multiple stories around the same central concept. It is useful if you have several disconnected stories that can all convey a single message, thus demonstrating the true importance of the message.

Storytelling, like classical rhetorical discourse, is also a dynamic process, structured in phases, which in fact are so generally distinct:

1. Searching: the research phase.
2. Sorting: the ordering and selection of elements that can bring an authentic and, at the same time, effective story to life.
3. Shaping: the elements or stories that have been selected are analyzed and shaped according to the needs and narrative patterns that you want to adopt.
4. Showing: this is the stage where the story is staged.
5. Sharing: is the sharing of narrated content.

This is how storytelling is configured as the art of communicating by telling stories. Storytelling or narration, therefore, is a communicative act that takes on different forms depending on what it exposes and depending on the tools chosen. Umberto Eco reminds us that stories, fairy tales, novels, novellas, gossip, etc. can be told through a film, a comic strip, an email, a photo story, a cycle of frescoes, the radio, the theatrical experience and so on.

In fact, in the last two hundred years the "narrative issue" has exploded leading to the birth of new disciplines: discourse analysis, narratology and semiotics. These have tried, from different points of view, to answer the question of how to say and communicate concepts. It is thanks to these disciplines that today we can talk about storytelling.

Storytelling becomes even more central if we think – we move into the realm of marketing – that people are no longer interested in buying products, but rather the stories that these products represent. In the same way, they no longer buy brands but the archetypes and myths that these brands allude to. In this sense, the product does not even need to be presented: it becomes more important to sell the idea than the product itself.

On top of this we should add a consideration on the emergence, even more recent, of digital storytelling. The main difference between traditional storytelling in the current classic mass media (cinema and television above all) and digital storytelling obviously lies in the medium itself and in the possibilities offered by digital aesthetics with respect to other types of media; in particular, when it comes to interactivity.

The argumentation

Focusing on the heart of any speech, the *demonstratio* or argumentation is precisely the fundamental aspect of a specific part of rhetorical discourse called *inventio* ('discovery, finding' of the arguments suitable to make a thesis reliable). In an argumentation, the "evidence" in support of one's own thesis is put forward and that of any opponents is contested. In short, it is the logical-argumentative part of any discourse; exactly, the one in which logical reasoning is carried out.

Logical reasoning is the cognitive process through which, starting from certain premises and making use of logical procedures, a conclusion is reached and – as a rule – represents the basis of any manifestation of thought, whether political or philosophical or even simply every day and informal thoughts.

The techniques through which one proceeds in logical reasoning are "arguments", by which one can show that, given certain premises, a conclusion is true or false. An argumentation consists of a sequence of logical propositions, one of which is understood as a conclusion flowing from the others, and which – in turn – becomes a premise for other arguments. Both the premises and the conclusion are assertions and can be true or false. In other words, reasoning means inferring conclusions from what one believes to be true and doing so according to laws or rules governing the validity of such deductive procedures.

Reasoning can be based on deductive, inductive, or abductive logic.

Reasoning is defined **deductive** when, knowing the premises and the laws that govern a phenomenon, it comes to a logical conclusion in line with the given premises: therefore, from general to particular. This is precisely the Aristotelian logic, the so-called syllogism.

The **syllogism** is the fundamental form of logical argumentation, consisting of three declarative propositions connected in such a way that from the first two, taken as premises, a conclusion can be deduced. A classic example of a syllogism (and deductive logic) is as follows:

1) All men are mortal;
2) All Greeks are men;
3) Therefore all Greeks are mortal.

The middle term 'men' is the one that, connected to the first premise, allows the conclusion to be reached.

Here we are faced with an example made with unequivocally true data; and indeed we speak of a mere syllogism. However, we speak of rhetorical syllogism or enthymeme when its premises are not necessarily 'true' but 'plausible'. The speaker, in fact, when arguing (in the *demonstratio* or demonstration) uses a form of syllogism that starts from premises that are not absolutely certain but plausible, and produces a conclusion that is equally not certain but plausible. The more the speaker is able to identify plausible arguments, the more they will have the possibility to argue effectively and persuade the audience.

Thus, for rhetoric (and for the speaker who makes use of it), the proofs of reasoning (or evidential arguments) consist of enthymemes, that is, syllogisms whose premises are not necessarily 'true' but 'plausible'.

However, the enthymeme should be kept distinct from the **argumentative fallacy**: we speak of a fallacy when in an enthymeme the premise (omitted) is false. An enthymeme (unlike a fallacy) does not deal with imperfection but with the implicit, in order to become faster, pleasant, allusive, curious. For example, it is particularly used in the field of advertising (where precisely we also speak of visual enthymeme).

In addition, we can state that an **inductive reasoning** is instead when, knowing the premises and the results of the reasoning, we intend to reconstruct the rules that allow it. In this case one goes from the particular to the general, and the conclusion may be false even though all the premises are true. An example of inductive reasoning is the following syllogism:

1) the website of a well-known press agency published some news that later turned out not to be true;
2) A friend of mine told me that another news was also false;
3) Therefore, all news from that agency is false.

Finally, a reasoning is considered **abductive**, when, knowing the rules and the results, one tries to reconstruct the premises. This is the logic used by the investigator who should reconstruct an initial situation, knowing the result obtained as a result of a causal link based on a scientific or probabilistic law. This reconstruction is obviously never certain but is valid only with a given level of probability. Concrete examples of abductive reasoning can be found in games such as master mind and naval battle.

The arrangement of topics

It is the part of rhetoric that codifies strategies for establishing the order of a discourse in its various aspects: for arranging parts in succession; for ordering words within a single sentence; for recounting a series of events in a clear, brief, and compelling way; or for organizing the arrangement of arguments to support a thesis.

Relative to this last purpose, classical rhetoric encodes three possible patterns to arrange topics. The first consists in placing the most solid ones at the end of the speech: it is the so-called **ascending order**. In this way, the audience brings with them, at the end of the speech, the memory of the last and most incisive evidence. However, one runs the risk of boring the audience at the beginning, of losing credibility because of the weakness of the initial arguments: in short, of losing the audience behind.

The second pattern would be to start with the strongest arguments and work your way **down to** the weakest, in a **descending order**. This scheme, however, makes it more difficult to disguise the less effective arguments: placed at the end of the argument, the audience will remember them better and, indeed, may perhaps end up remembering only those.

The third model, called Homeric order or **Nestorian order** (from the arrangement in the shape of pincers with which Nestor, in the fourth book of the Iliad, had lined up the Greek troops in battle), represents a synthesis of the two previous ones, of which it aims to achieve the merits and avoid the defects. It consists in fact in distributing the more fragile arguments in the middle, and the more persuasive ones at the beginning and end of the evidential speech. In this way the speaker will not risk losing authority or boring the audience and, at the same time, they will make sure that the strong arguments that they have set aside for the final part will be remembered because of their effectiveness.

However, we should be paying attention to a further aspect. The speaker, in their oral discourse, should always consider how the audience's behavior will be affected by the speech: they should be able to grasp and evaluate any changes in behavior, gradually reworking the arrangement of the arguments accordingly in a sort of necessary and permanent adjustment.

The virtues of a speech

Ancient rhetoricians speak of *virtutes elocutionis* to indicate the virtues that a persuasive speech necessarily had to possess.

These are: *àptum* (appropriateness), *pùritas* (lexical and grammatical correctness), *perspicùitas* (clarity), *ornàtus* (elegance).

A speech should first of all be appropriate to the purpose and circumstances (*aptum*). This quality includes the need to choose words that reflect the nature of things (truthful speech) and that do not offend the moral sense of the audience (decent speech).

Abiding by lexical and grammatical norms (*puritas*) ensures the linguistic comprehensibility of a speech. This virtue requires the use of words, syntactic constructs and expressions that conform to current and possibly specialized use. Faced with a possible conflict between grammar and rhetoric, the latter is preferred (and the rhetorical figures typical of the *ornatus*, which can sometimes force the correct grammatical and lexical structure).

The *ornatus* codifies precisely the artistic and aesthetic aspects of the rhetorical discourse. It is considered an important requirement, although formally accessory, that over the centuries has developed in a hypertrophic way. However, in recent decades has occupied the entire field of the discipline and has led to talk of a “restricted” rhetoric, conceived as a technique of verbal expression only.

Clarity

The last requirement is that of clarity (*perspicuitas*): it guarantees the general comprehensibility of the speech and safeguards the argumentative intention of the speaker from any risk of misunderstanding. It is first and foremost a reflection of the clarity of thoughts: the level of *inventio* should always be reflected in that of *elocutio*. The risks to be avoided are represented by semantic ambiguity and syntactic ambiguity (particularly present, as we shall see, in argumentative fallacies). The corresponding error by default is obscurity but – note well – obscure speech is also unintelligible because it is delivered with insufficient volume of voice, with confused diction, etc.

We will speak again about the tools to bring intelligibility to a speech in the chapter devoted to the pitfalls of (not only) written speech.

Brevity

Among the various types of beginnings of a speech we have mentioned, in addition to the affectation of modesty or declaration of inadequacy (which consists in confessing one's own inadequacy and is considered an effective tool because it tends to raise sympathy towards those in difficulty), also the declaration of brevity.

Exemplified by the "I'll be brief" of many speeches, even modern ones, it is an instrument used enormously in every context. The speaker, in these cases, almost seems to want to reassure the audience that listening will be the minimum requirement and that they will soon be able to return to more useful and pleasant things. This is probably one of the crudest and most ineffective way to begin a speech and empathize with those who read or listen, yet practiced as an immortal *cliché*.

Brevity, especially in recent years, has become a gospel: pursued with various (and often inadequate) tools, it appears objectively elusive, often imposed without fully understanding its meaning and, therefore, mostly unrealized.

Instead, the reference to brevity should take us elsewhere: precisely to the search for the essential. What is it and how is it achieved? First of all, let's move away from quantitative approaches to a requirement that is essentially qualitative: we cannot 'quantify' what may be necessary and sufficient ('quality') by measuring time or space ('quantity'). Theoretically, we cannot force anyone (ourselves and others, in any context) to carry out a 'discourse' in a predetermined time or number of pages or characters, regardless of any further need and evaluation. This would be an illogical and unfair solution, and moreover, ephemeral.

Of course, we also need to understand how the need to impose (albeit improperly) a generic 'conciseness' or 'brevity' in many contexts is the result of a very unpleasant perception of the typical speaker of the last few decades. Let's admit it: the average Italian speaker is a charming storyteller, a great joker, but a confused and ineffective communicator; quite different, for example, from the American or the German speaker, who are much more essential and direct in their communication.

And so the Italian listener defends themselves, in many contexts, by imposing rules and limits to the waste of time and boredom caused by the Italian speaker: from the *manager* who asks their subordinates to be concise, to the judge who invites the lawyer to be brief, to the journalist who cuts off the interviewee who exaggerates. The additional problem is that, often, in some contexts, this is done by imposing quantitative limits (minutes in the case of speaking, pages or even characters in the case of writing).

Whether it is a job interview or a criminal trial, the Italian listener defends themselves from what they fear the most: the Italian speaker and the fact that they do not conclude. Some authors, in the face of such a strong and current need to "contain" (within precise margins) written and oral speech, in all contexts, rightly speak of "emphasizing banality", explaining how, from a linguistic and logical-argumentative point of view, the opposite of "synthetic" is not "verbose" but "analytical". And so, since an analytical discourse can be clear while a synthetic discourse can still be obscure, 'conciseness' may not be sufficient at all for a good argument.

In short: it is not necessarily the case that a speech, in order to be synthetic, should also be brief. Therefore, the problem of synthesis certainly cannot be solved by "giving numbers", that is, by indicating or even imposing quantitative criteria.

In reality, the only possible solution is cultural. We need precise training to make people understand that the search for what is essential starts precisely from the correct identification of the basic elements of a discourse, and from their equally correct and effective arrangement and transmission.

The knowledge (at least basic) of grammar and rhetoric can allow any of us to understand that a speech cannot be a series of elements piled up but an organic design, a complete and semantically cohesive entirety. A carefully chosen and organized content should then correspond to an adequate linguistic and expressive form, which the ancient rhetoricians called precisely 'elocution' (*elocutio*) and within which there is also room for the so-called figurative language (the one, to be clear, that makes use of rhetorical figures).

However, the rules exist as long as there is someone who violates them: therefore, until we have individuals who can speak and write correctly, briefly and effectively, unfortunately there will always be a need for corrective measures and impositions, quantitative even where the *deficit* is qualitative.

So, for many years to come, we will still have to put up with the demand to be brief no matter what, and also with the imposition of several characters or pages or minutes to expound or communicate something. And yet, those who – even in the absence of "mass training" – have developed sensitivity and adequate knowledge in the field of logic and rhetoric, will still be able to make use of brevity, succeeding better than others in responding to any context and oratorical need: that is, communicating correctly, briefly and effectively.

THE FIGURATIVE LANGUAGE

Words and their meaning

In the context of persuasive (rhetorical) discourse, rhetorical figures represent an extremely flexible and powerful tool. If the argument is the nail, the figure is the way to stick it in, Olivier Reboul reminds us.

With the rhetorical figures we are in the *elocutio* (or elocution), that is, one of the parts of a rhetorical discourse consisting of the act of giving linguistic form to ideas. The *elocutio* identifies and teaches the strategies to construct a linguistic formulation appropriate to the arguments found thanks to the *inventio* (discovery) and placed according to an appropriate *dispositio* (arrangement).

It is now necessary to highlight the fact that each **word** contains two elements:

- **signifier**: the letters and sounds that constitute it, so it is the sound of the word or its spelling;
- **signified**: the image or information that the word transfers to us, that is, the meaning we give to a graphic symbol or sound.

Meaning, in turn, can be:

- **denotative:** literal, primary and objective, principal and commonly spread and shared,
- **connotative:** unusual, uncommon or figurative; words are understood in their allusive and therefore subjective meaning; the psychological aspect associated with the term.

In the same way, the word 'desert' can indicate a geographical place (denotation) or a human condition (connotation: the desert of the soul, solitude).

The denotative meaning is used in ordinary communication, to describe and inform; instead the connotative meaning is used to add extra value to a word, enriching the word itself and increasing the expressive effectiveness of the language.

Denotation is, therefore, the literal meaning of a term; connotation is its emotional content, with all its possible suggestions. Thus, in vocabularies, the first meaning given is the denotative one, followed by the connotative ones, referred to as figurative meanings.

Connotative language and rhetorical figures

The use of language in its connotative meaning is called figurative language, which makes use of **rhetorical figures.** These figures are nothing else than stylistic procedures used in speech: schemes (in Greek *schêma* means 'configuration, figure' – in fact they are expressive schemes) according to which the expression of thought can be shaped. In practice, they transform the elementary and literal thought, leading the reader or listener 'elsewhere': if well crafted, they lead them exactly where the speaker wants. For example, with the metaphor "John is a lion" the speaker certainly does not intend to claim that John is a quadruped with tail and mane, but they want to convey a concept that goes beyond the literal meaning, with greater effectiveness and less expenditure of words and energy than the possible use of a paraphrase ("John has a courage that is typical of lions").

There is more: with the appropriate use of certain rhetorical figures (such as, for example, anaphora and epiphora) you can then create a complex and harmonious structure of connected sentences, but also of well-connected thoughts, strengthening the textual cohesion and enhancing the entire communicative context.

In short, rhetorical figures are not just the 'form' to be given to the thoughts themselves, but they help to give substance to any discourse.

Not all figures, however, are 'rhetorical', let's be clear: for example, there are also poetic, humorous or simply lexical ones. A rhetorical figure, however, always aims to persuade, even when it apparently violates the rules of syntax or grammar. In fact, a repetition of elements can represent a defect of a speech, but also a rhetorical tool to give it a *surplus* meaning. And only in this case syntax and grammar are put aside.

The modern systematization of rhetorical figures identifies two general classes of discourse patterns: figures that operate on single words and figures that operate instead on word connections. Figures that operate on the single word are identified in **tropes** (or metaphors). Its etymology (*trópos* in Greek means 'direction') shows that it is a 'turn' given to an expression that is 'diverted' from its original content to cover another content.

Figures that operate on the connection of words are divided into two groups: **figures of speech** (which concern the artificial disposition of elements) and **figures of thought** (which model the contents of speech and are real schemes). Figures are then distinguished based on their generative principles, that is, based on the different procedures that give rise to each of them: deduction, addition, substitution, permutation (with the clarification that, for figures operating on single words, the only possible category is obviously only that of 'substitution': the proper term is in fact replaced by a synonym or a trope).

When to use rhetorical figures

The list of situations in which the use of rhetorical figures could be useful is endless. For example, from amplifying concepts or elements (anaphora, anadiplosis, diaphora, *climax*, emphasis, epanalepsis, hyperbole etc.) to attenuating them (ellipsis, euphemism, periphrasis etc.), from opposing (antithesis, oxymoron, paradox) to simulating (antiphrasis, irony, litotes).

However, it is essential to evaluate the audience and their knowledge and feelings shared with the speaker (an irony made in an inappropriate context, or one that presupposes cultural knowledge not possessed by the audience, will not only fail to achieve the objective but will also irreparably damage the continuation of the speech and the image of the speaker).

There is also the limitation represented by the knowledge and ability to use these tools with balance and respect for others.

Some fundamental rhetorical figures will be analyzed

below, grouped according to the function-objective that in the context of a discourse (written or oral) they might play.

To amplify

To amplify means to expand in breadth and intensity both the subject matter of a speech (i.e., with data, arguments, opinions, etc.) and a single expression. The result of amplification, according to rhetoric, is the enrichment of ideas and the intensification of emotions to reach the audience more easily and remain imprinted in their memory.

Amplification can be rendered first and foremost through **emphasis** (from the Greek 'I show'). On a literal level, the emphatic sentence affirms data that is in fact already evident, if not sometimes even banal.

With emphasis, as with many other rhetorical figures, the reader or listener is invited to follow the speaker: collaboration is asked in order to move 'elsewhere' and be able to grasp the full meaning that is hidden behind the use of a word or expression.

Sometimes emphasis is also accomplished very effectively through the repetition of one or more elements. Take the expression "a child is just a *child*."

Here, too, the information is evident. The expression, therefore, induces one to pause on the *surplus* meaning that it brings with it: weakness, unreliability, innocence, the right to indulgent treatment, etc. *Surplus* that is thus made far more visible than a longer and less effective analytical description of the type:

> "a child may not perceive the disvalue of his or her actions given the not-yet-advanced development of his or her abilities."

However, emphasis is achieved through the repetition of a term (*child*) and, in fact, through another rhetorical figure: the **diaphora.** This is realized when a word within the same textual segment is repeated but assuming a different meaning (and precisely, in the second occurrence, with in an emphatic way): "a father is always a *father*"; "business is *business*".

Like all rhetorical figures of repetition (anaphora, epiphora, epanalepsis, anadiplosis), the diaphora lets differences emerge where it seems to establish identity.

Finally, in the figurative arts a true manifesto of emphasis is represented by a masterpiece by Munch (*The Scream*, 1893, National Gallery, Oslo), with that central figure distorted in terror that spreads like psychic waves throughout the landscape. A representation capable of condensing into a single image the deformation of reality produced by the sense of anguish and at the same time the unbearable pressure that the external world exerts on the individual, to the point of deforming him into a grotesque mask.

The danger that the emphasis may not be understood, causing a trivialization of the sentence (or, better, causing the addressee to just understand the literal sense), induces the speaker – in speech – to emphasize it also with means that are above all phonetic-prosodic (related, that is, to the sound-modulation of the voice): peaks of accent, increase of speed, vocalic lengthening, dosage of pauses. And all can be accompanied by proxemic indices (e.g., specific gestures).

Some guarantee seems to be given, in writing-transcription, using the capital letter. But, on closer inspection, this is a way of achieving emphasis and gaining the attention of the addressee that is not only grammatically incorrect, but even trivial and at the same time unpleasant (some commentator has sharply spoken of 'capitalization', and we will discuss this in connection with the pitfalls of especially written speech).

But amplification can also be achieved through **hyperbole**. From the Greek 'I throw ', 'I exceed', it consists in taking the meaning of an expression to excess, amplifying or reducing its reference to reality in order to reinforce its meaning and increase, by contrast, its credibility: "I walked a million miles to get here", "I died of embarrassment", I'm so hungry I could eat a horse", "She's as old as the hills".

Traditionally, hyperbole coincides with exaggeration, i.e., favoring a sentence in which the reference to reality is rendered unbelievable in order to intensify the original expression to the maximum or minimum degree, with effects of various kinds, even ironic and paradoxical. It is precisely the improbability of the entire phrase to induce the recipient to look for a sense other than the literal one. Hyperbole serves to increase or decrease something beyond the truth, but it is a "lie" that does not want to deceive: to achieve it, it is necessary to deform reality, without betraying it.

In mass culture, hyperbole is widely used in advertising texts. Contemporary advertising also uses hyperbole on a visual level, coming close to an artistic trend that exploits the macro and the micro to create sense effects. More generally, hyperbole is combined with metaphor, which becomes hyperbolic, as in numerous advertisements.

There is also a two-faced rhetorical figure, the **litotes**, because it can obtain both the effect of amplification and the opposite effect of attenuation. In Greek 'simplicity', it is a figure that affirms through the negation of the opposite. For example, "it is not small" to say that it is large.

The procedure is that of the periphrasis (the litotes is a form of periphrasis) and the purpose is to express in an attenuated way what one wants to let be understood, and of which one wants to confirm all the strength. Often the litotes is a **euphemistic periphrasis**, in which the harshness of an expression is softened: "he is not a genius", avoiding saying "he is an idiot".

But even more often, the effect is primarily ironic. In fact, the litotes does not have its own specific form, but rather represents a formula of passage between different rhetorical schemes, combined in a single verbal segment. For example, with the expression "he is not an Adonis" we do not simply mean that a subject is not particularly beautiful, but rather that he is certainly ugly. Thus, the litotes approaches irony (and more precisely, the irony of dissimulation). If, then, the statement to the contrary takes on a superlative degree, the figure also approaches hyperbole. It will be up to the addressee, based on the analysis of the context, to attribute to the expression the value of mitigation, interpreting it in a euphemistic sense, or the value of reinforcement, interpreting it in an emphatic or hyperbolic sense. This is also why we sometimes speak of a 'two-faced' figure.

The litotes is therefore characterized by this decisive responsibility of the addressee in assigning it one or another of the possible meaning (euphemism, hyperbole, irony). Its function will therefore depend on the argumentative development of the discourse, the context and the ability of the addressee (to know the relevant circumstances of reality). Keeping in mind that with hyperbole a paradoxical limit is recalled, situated beyond the threshold of possibility (whose very improbability or absurdity invites the addressee to divert attention from the literal datum in order to orient it however within the threshold of possibility), while with the litotes the limit is recalled only to be immediately denied and to act as a catapult because the thought takes the direction wanted by the speaker.

Further rhetorical tools to obtain the amplification of the message are certainly the main **figures of repetition** (or accumulation): anaphora, epiphora, diaphora (which we have already seen to achieve different emphasis), epanalepsis, anadiplosis, symploce.

Rhetorical repetition consists in using the same element at different points in the sentence or discourse. But only when one of these needs has to be satisfied: to facilitate connections between parts of the text that are distant from each other (thus favoring textual cohesion and comprehension of the whole) or to enrich (in the sense of embellishing) a discourse. Only when they have these functions, repetitions are neither superfluous nor cumbersome and are precisely considered 'rhetorical'.

For example, figures such as the anaphora or the epiphora are particularly frequent in public discourse and are used to give greater effectiveness to the discourse. These figures mainly concern the lexical level: they transmit 'images' that give the words used expressive values that go beyond the current one, generating in the interlocutor a sort of 'estrangement'.

Anaphora (from the Greek 'I carry back') is the figure of insistence: it consists precisely in the repetition of a word or a group of words at the beginning of a sentence or verse (so-called textual segment), according to the following scheme: /x... /x.../. The classic example of anaphora is Dantesque and can help us to better understand when a repetition does not represent an error but an added value:

"*Through me is the way to the city of woe.*
Through me is the way to sorrow eternal.
Through me is the way to the lost below."
(Dante, *The Divine Comedy*, *Inferno*, III, 1-3)

Another no less famous anaphora is, however, "*I have a dream*" (repeated 9 times) in the historic speech delivered by Martin Luther King Jr. on August 28, 1963 in front of the Lincoln Memorial in Washington at the conclusion of the march in favor of civil rights. It remains one of the most studied and cloned rhetorical examples.

Numerous contemporary speakers have also made use of it. Think of Barack Obama, who often made use of the anaphora used in ternary rhythm:

"*No* bailouts, *no* handouts, and *no* copouts."
(Barack Obama, State of the Union address, 2012)

"This country has more wealth than any nation, *but that's not what* makes us rich. We have the most powerful military in history, *but that's not what* makes us strong. Our university, our culture are all the envy of the world, *but that's not what* keeps the world coming to our shores."
(Barack Obama, re-election speech, 2012).

And, even more recently, the speech given on April 5, 2020 by Queen Elizabeth II (during the Covid-19 outbreak):

> "*We will* be with our friends *again*, *we will* be with our families *again*; *we will* meet *again*."

with a perfect integration of anaphora in ternary rhythm (at the beginning of the textual segments) and epiphora (at the end of the segments). From the Greek 'to bring upon', the **epiphora** is a mirror image of the anaphora and consists of the repetition of a word or a group of words at the end of a textual segment, according to the scheme: /*...x*/*...x*/. As in the following example:

> "The man went out *drunk,* came back *drunk*, woke up *drunk*."

Like the anaphora, the final recovery characterizes different types of speech that make use (albeit with different communicative purposes) of parallelisms. In the oratorical technique, it is generally aimed at raising the register of the dictation and capturing attention.

The combination of anaphora and epiphora generates the additional figure of **symploce**, where the beginning and end of a sentence of any length can become the beginning or end of one or more subsequent sentences according to the different pattern: /x...*y*/*x*...*y*/. For example:

> "*Let us beware* of envious man, *always*; *let us* also *beware* of envying man, *always*."

Then there is also **epanalepsis**: from the Greek 'I repeat', it consists in the consecutive repetition (doubling) of a word or a group of words or at the beginning of a textual segment – according to the pattern /aa.../:

"I *know*, I *know:* I repeat things."

or in the middle, according to the pattern */...aa.../*:

"Of course – I *know* – I repeat things."

Like the other figures of repetition, the epanalepsis aims to highlight already formulated concepts that, through iteration, can draw the attention and imprint themselves more easily in the memory of the audience.

What, however, can often characterize the use of rhetorical figures of repetition, and can prove to be a fundamental additive, is the use (as we have seen in many of the examples reported) of symmetry in the repetition. The **isocolon** indicates precisely the perfect symmetry between two or more members of a verbal segment in terms of number of words, syntactic structure and rhythm. If there are two members, we speak of bipartition. Three-member parallelism is called ***tricolon*** (or also **ternary rhythm**). The classic example is from Caesar:

"Veni, vidi, vici."

But you can also have four members and in this case we speak of quadrature or ***tetracolon***. However, the *tricolon*, more commonly called **ternary rhythm**, is the one mainly used and it consists precisely in the reiteration of three elements. The preference towards the ternary rhythm is due to the fact that from the rhythmic point of view the accumulations with more than three members can be weak by excess, while the binary structures (i.e., accumulations with only two members) can be weak by default. Ternary structures, on the other hand, seem to be the most harmonious and balanced (with a center and two extremes).

Finally, amplification can also be achieved using *climax*. Also known as gradation or ascending gradation, it consists in moving gradually from one concept to another, or in reiterating a single concept with synonymous words that are gradually more effective and intense, or more generally in arranging the terms of a sentence in increasing order of value and strength. For example:

> "I will simply show how something was missing in this matter, the premise, the development – everything!"

Curiosity: the original Greek term (but also the Latin one) is feminine and becomes over time, in common use, masculine (the use of the feminine is instead relegated to rhetorical specialist use).

The oldest scheme of the *climax* is that of a continuous anadiplosis according to the following scheme: *...x/x...y/y...z/z...* One proceeds precisely by 'steps' (the word *climax* means precisely 'staircase'), stopping on each before climbing the next; and each 'step' on which one stops becomes the first of the next sentence. In order to increase the intensity and give emphasis to a speech, one writes and speaks, therefore, as one climbs the stairs: at each word, at each expression one gives a little more strength to the speech, one chooses words that become more and more intense, as it happens when one climbs and each step of the staircase is a little higher, bringing with it a little more emphasis than the previous one. The emotion of those who read or listen grows along with the words: after each comma there is something stronger waiting for them.

But stairs can also be descended. In fact, descending is sometimes the only thing to do when you have reached the top, especially in contexts where it is then appropriate to lighten the tone. There is also the opposite of the climax, the descent from the emphasis, the deflation: it is the ***anticlimax***. Here, too, we work on the intensity of the discourse, but in the opposite way: we aim to remove, to soften. And so the intensity of the speech gradually lowers; for example:

> "She no longer had the strength to fight him and stood there, silent, unmoving."

To compare

Sometimes there may be a need to highlight a contrast or literally oppose a thesis or an opponent. On the verbal level, one can resort first to the **antithesis**. It is a figure that consists in the contrast (same as the Greek etymology) of ideas expressed by putting in correspondence words (or segments of text) of opposite or contrasting meaning, or more or less clear conceptual polarities: for example, the use of the concepts of life/death, beautiful/ugly, day/night etc. The terms placed in opposition should, however, have a common aspect, or belong to the same semantic field. The purpose is to reinforce the concept expressed. For example:

> "he worked during the day, *not at night.*"

More creative, however, is the **oxymoron**. The Greek etymology identifies what is "acutely insane, wittily senseless", and the figure consists in fact in joining two words or expressions that are irreconcilable in meaning, as they properly indicate an antithesis or contrariety. Same as the antithesis, the oxymoron unites, by contrasting them, two thoughts or two meanings that are in themselves irreconcilable because one expresses the opposite of the other. For example, in everyday use: "awfully good," "bittersweet," "same difference", "alone together", and "original copy".

The oxymoron differs from antithesis in that, instead of emphasizing the opposition between contrary terms, it predicts their paradoxical coincidence (and coexistence). In the oxymoron, two ideas that are normally kept apart because they are irreconcilable are brought together to produce an unexpected (short) circuit that gives them a surprising "energy of sense" that can strike the listener or the reader. It is therefore a game of intelligence, whose main ingredient is surprise.

Currently, the oxymoron appears with a certain frequency in the language of advertising and in that of politics and political propaganda. In short, the oxymoron has become widespread, in any context.

But the contrast can also be achieved with other rhetorical figures that imply the use of non-verbal communication, such as the **apostrophe.** It derives its name from the gesture of the speaker who, ceasing to address their audience (metaphorically turning their back on them – from the Greek 'I turn away'), addresses to a new interlocutor, usually the opponent (or some other person present in the room – but it can also be directed to abstract or collective entities). By means of the apostrophe, the speech undergoes an abrupt change both linguistically (with the transition to the imperative or the vocative), as well as its point of view and focus, and its tone (the degree of emotional intensity is greater). Since ancient times, it has aimed to blatantly express the sensitivity of the speaker, with the intention of raising *pathos* and, consequently, a sympathetic reaction from the audience.

To Simulate

It is not always the intention of the speaker to 'counter' or 'oppose'. Much more often they have the need to convey a message that is not obvious or to convey a different impression or feeling to the audience or opponent in order to surprise them later.

Simulation-dissimulation can then be particularly useful. **Simulation** is first of all a figure similar to irony: in fact, in the ancient rhetoric a figure called "irony of simulation" was created, a very frequent form of refutation in Socratic dialogues. Since Socrates declares "all I know is that I know nothing", none of his refutations can be based on the opposition of his own truth (that Socrates recognizes precisely not to possess) to the truth declared by his interlocutor. How can we then demonstrate the falsity of an affirmation without opposing to it a true one? Socrates applies a method of discussion that relies only on what the interlocutor affirms, accepts and recognizes by themselves: after having asked the interlocutor to express themselves explicitly and clearly on what they 'believe to be true' around a certain theme, he proceeds by deriving from the interlocutor's thesis all possible consequences, and highlighting those in a broad sense that are unreasonable, and of which the interlocutor was evidently unaware, thus ending up by demonstrating the irrationality of the starting thesis, and 'ridiculing' the interlocutor..

Therefore simulation technically consists in pretending to support a different thesis from your own one; apparently sharing the positions of the adversary first to raise within the audience an emotional reaction of surprise and opposition, and then to highlight the weak aspects and to show that the acceptance of such positions would carry to unacceptable consequences, ending also by ridiculing the same interlocutor. It should also be said that the functions that the ridicule has in the argumentation are similar to those of the absurd in the logical-mathematical demonstration: to reduce to ridicule is to reduce to absurdity. In fact, it consists in momentarily accepting the "principles" of the opposite thesis, in order to reject its conclusions because absurd (simulation), and therefore to deny the admissibility of the thesis itself (for inconsistency between the stated premises and the conclusions).

The **argumentation for absurdity** can take two different forms depending on whether we want to prove the truth or simply the falsity of a given proposition. Different from the demonstration by absurdity, properly called proof by absurdity (which demonstrates the truth of a proposition by the false consequences that derive from its contradictory) is the **reduction to absurdity** which demonstrates the falsity of a proposition by showing the false consequences to which it logically leads. In fact, there is great affinity between the two forms of argumentation: the only difference is that in the proof by absurdity there is the hypothetical assumption of the contradictory premise, which does not happen in the reduction to absurdity. Indeed, the latter is ultimately the other part of the proof by absurdity, namely the syllogistic deduction of the false proposition.

On the other hand, dissimulation occurs when the speaker hides (dissimulates) their own thoughts through a systematic use of figures of attenuation (the litotes, in particular) or in using interrogative formulas showing apparent uncertainty (and dissimulating, therefore, their own conviction – so called Socratic irony).

However, dissimulation can also be achieved through other means, such as the use of "affected modesty" (or **affectation of modesty**), through which the speaker performs (simulates) a (fake and ostentatious) downgrading of their authority or ability as well as their opinion. The category of these simulated forms of humility (understatement, we might say) also includes the "plural of modesty" or the impersonal.

In order to understand irony, however, it is necessary to start from the **antiphrasis**, which is its essential and most open form, limited to a single expression and consisting in saying something while meaning the opposite. For example: "What a beautiful day!" (while it's raining cats and dogs). It is therefore based on an extremely simple and visible mechanism of sense inversion, relying on immediate contextual disambiguation (clarification). A U-turn of sense can concern both the propositional part ("He has some brilliant ideas", meaning instead that they are trivial) and the strength given even to a single expression ("Try!", in the sense of challenge; or again: "Congratulations!" – in an ironic sense).

Irony, on the other hand, is a more complex, subtle and nuanced form of antiphrasis (i.e., semantic inversion), consisting in saying the opposite of what one believes and what it really is, but in such a way as to make clear one's intention and therefore not allowing the audience to misunderstand the thesis the speaker really intends to support. Irony is the art of striking without striking, of hiding in order to astutely attack, according to the norm of the fox (an 'ironic' animal, simulator by nature, as suggested by the Greek etymology of the word: irony is of 'who questions by pretending not to know'). It is a sword that wounds but does not kill, and yet can hurt more than a direct insult.

Irony is therefore certainly different from **lying** because the intentionally false statement is used to communicate something that the speaker considers true. Decisive to trigger irony (and its understanding) is the possibility of the interlocutors to refer to shared knowledge and evaluations, to basic assumptions and expectations on the communicative modernized situation. Therefore, by constructing an ironic message the author has to be aware of the reasons why irony is used, of the context in which it is applied and of the target audience, which should be able to accept and understand the choice of medium and the message conveyed (and should therefore share with the speaker a common heritage of knowledge and skills). It is also argued that ironic statements are 'echoic' representations of one's own opinions (self-irony) or those of others: through irony, the speaker reproduces (almost echoing) a worldview, to express their position (of distance, disapproval or derision) with respect to it.

Some non-verbal signals play a decisive role in ironic communication: prosodic (the so-called ironic intonation), mimicry and proxemics. These signals can be integrated and represent precise indexes of recognition, favoring the recipient. Also because – it should be underlined – the audience should be absolutely able to understand it: irony is a rhetorical figure that requires a certain kind of understanding, it is autonomous and it would not be the same if one was to explain it. As soon as a word of explanation is added, irony is destroyed.

Studies in evolutionary psychology have long noted that understanding irony requires a complex interweaving of brain development, cognitive abilities, and social-cognitive experiences. The development of the brain areas involved in this process matures over long periods of time and differs from person to person. The results of some of the earliest studies on the understanding of irony (in the 1980s) showed that at the age of 6, children were able to understand sincere acts of communication without problems, understanding of deception improved between the ages of 6 and 13, and finally understanding of irony began at the age of 13 (indeed, the data also showed that in adults irony was understood in only 50% of cases...).

Different from irony – although mistakenly confused with it – is **sarcasm**. The term derives from Greek (it refers to tear, bite, strip off the flesh) and the etymology helps to easily understand its intrinsic meaning: it is in fact a form of bitter and pungent irony, inspired by animosity and therefore intended to offend and humiliate. Some linguistics experts consider it a "polite insult". And the difference between irony and sarcasm is between what makes one smile and what instead hurts.

There is a fine line, and the substantial differences can be recognized by the effect they produce. Irony has a beneficial effect, almost relaxing: it dissipates tensions, stimulates new thoughts and even if it is used to express disappointment, it is generally expressed with a benevolent spirit. Irony presupposes creativity and, if well dosed, it is positive because it allows you to get out of an adverse mood and resize the scope, relativizing the facts. Irony tends mainly to lighten the scenario and the comparison. Sarcasm, on the other hand, wounds severely. The goal of sarcasm is to sting, to make one feel guilty, to provoke negative reactions in order to achieve a personal goal, if only to keep the other under psychological control. Sarcasm is irony taken to excess and moved by the purpose of diminishing and undervaluing the other.

Sarcasm, then, involves the presence of primitive, often unconscious, aggressive impulses and is a tool of the weak who wants to appear strong and attack hard, ensuring that they will not be attacked (because they have acted as a joke). "Freedom begins with irony," said Victor Hugo. But using irony is not for everyone: it's a serious thing, to be used wisely. If constructed or misused, it can become very dangerous, producing exactly opposite effects to expectations.

To create

One can be a particularly creative speaker by creating, whenever possible and appropriate, a **metaphor** with which to accompany, enhancing, one's communication. It is the best-known rhetorical figure and, at the same time, the most difficult to define (from the Greek "I transfer" – a transfer of meaning, we might add). Based on a canonical definition it consists of a replacement of a word by another whose literal sense has some resemblance to the literal sense of the replaced word. For example, "John is a lion," meaning he is courageous as a lion; and again, "a mountain of work," "a heart of stone", "you are my sunshine", "that place is a zoo", "the years fly by." All examples where nouns, adjectives, verbs and nominal predicates are used. Metaphor, therefore, can identify novel links between different aspects of reality.

But there is more. There is a direct relationship between the cognitive value of the figure and the aesthetic pleasure derived from it: we derive pleasure from metaphors because they allow us to discover situations that are not evident to us or that we do not think about. In a certain way metaphors can be compared to works of art: they represent the iconic equivalent of conceptual representation and connect intellectual speculation and the perceivable world.

In addition, with the **metonymy** we make good use of creativity, and we satisfy the need to imprint concepts differently expressed with more ordinary terms or expressions. According to the rhetorical tradition (the Greek term indicates a 'change of name'), it occurs when one designates any entity by means of the name of another entity that is to the first as the cause is to the effect and vice versa, or that corresponds to it by ties of mutual dependence: referring to the President of the United States or their administration as "the White House" or "the Oval Office"; referring to the American technology industry as "Silicon Valley"; referring to the American advertising industry as "Madison Avenue".

The **synecdoche** can have a similar effect and function. It consists in expressing a notion by means of another that is with the first in a relationship of quantitative order (from the Greek 'I receive together'). There are two types of synecdoche. With the generalizing synecdoche we name 'the more for the less', that is the wider concept to indicate the narrower one: "America" (to mean the United States of America). Instead with the particularizing synecdoche we name 'the less for the more', i.e., the narrower concept to mean the wider one. For example, the part for the whole: "Check out my new wheels" ("wheels" for a "car"). The synecdoche is not created by the individual but from a linguistic use regulated by cultural customs, and – like the metonymy – it acts in a constant way on the language, to the point of modifying the very system of the language, enriching its lexicon.

Finally, we should remember that the **synesthesia** represents a very special tool to give added value to our thinking. The etymology of the term already tells us a lot ('I feel together', therefore 'simultaneous sensation'). It is a type of metaphor that consists in associating terms that belong to different sensory spheres: visual, auditory, olfactory, tactile and gustatory ("thy voice is like wine to me" (Oscar Wilde, *Salome*). Two different sensory perceptions come together to create a new and expressively powerful image. In the examples "rough voice" or "warm color" the two terms refer to sensations of different types such as touch and hearing, touch and sight respectively. These juxtapositions create a sense of estrangement, with an effect typical of rhetorical figures such as the metaphor and also the oxymoron (as the words are irreconcilable from a sensorial point of view). Well known since ancient times, the synesthesia was not classified among discursive technicalities but referred to a specific mental experience of multisensory type, consisting of the ability to interpret a given sensation in terms of a sensation from another source (for example, Pythagoras associated numbers and sounds and Aristotle compared tastes, colors and sounds with touch).

To vary

Sometimes it may be necessary to avoid the repetition of a term or even a proper noun. *Variatio* is precisely the syntactic, lexical, grammatical, semantic or phonetic variation made to make a speech elegant, avoiding repetition (not rhetorically justified) or creating rhythmic-metrical movement.

It can be achieved, in fact, using certain figures such as first of all the **periphrasis** (or circumlocution). From the Greek "speak in a roundabout way", it consists in designating an object not with the term that usually denotes it but by means of a circumlocution that indicates certain qualities of it. For example, in Dante Alighieri "he who moves everything" to indicate God. However, unlike the definition (which makes explicit the essential properties of the object to be defined), the periphrasis highlights only the data that the speaker considers crucial with respect to the general context of their communication and their argumentative intention. The periphrasis is a rhetorical device to be used with different figures (euphemisms, lithotypes, metaphors, synecdoches, metonymies) and have some typical functions. It is used for verbal censorship and mitigation, useful for distancing oneself from realities (which are in any case 'told') that are not appropriate or necessary to deal with explicitly: they may, for example, concern sex, pain, death, or potentially 'difficult' themes. More simply, its stylistic function is certainly to avoid the repetition of a word already used.

The **antonomasia** is instead a form of periphrasis that assumes the equivalence between the proper name of an individual and certain characteristic qualities. It is, therefore, an equivalence between the whole and a part, similar to the synecdoche. For this reason, the antonomasia is considered a variant of the synecdoche that involves proper names. It can consist in the substitution of a proper name with a periphrasis or an epithet (for example: "the prince of darkness", "the hero of the two worlds"). Or – on the contrary – in the substitution of a common name with the proper name of a person who has distinguished themselves by the qualities designated by the epithet (for example, "a Judas" to mean a traitor).

Already in ancient rhetoric, the figure also has a very practical function: to avoid the repetition of a proper name (because it may be too close in the textual segment) and to obey possible censures (in some societies and contexts, the duty to avoid certain names considered taboo – think of Satan, also referred to as "the Evil One", "the prince of darkness"). The greater the cultural correspondence and adaptation between speaker and audience is, the more effective the figure is. The antonomasia represents stereotypes and for this reason it is subject to the particular historical and cultural context, and therefore it is able to originate and spread rapidly. This figure is widely used, especially in the language of journalism, and then destined to be forgotten over a few years.

To allude

Perhaps few people know that allusion is a real rhetorical figure. From the Latin 'game, joke' (and, therefore, 'playful speech'), it consists in referring, indirectly, to an event, a fact or a subject, without ever naming it explicitly.

Latin rhetoricians considered allusion a playful variant of the emphasis: in fact, the two figures have in common the fullness of meaning and the property of implying more than what they explicitly say. Also here, as in the emphasis, the addressee has to recognize the allusive reference. They will also have to reconstruct the implicit meaning of the figure based on the knowledge shared with the speaker. The speaker will then call upon this knowledge, true or only supposed, assuming the risks, similarly to other rhetorical figures (for example, irony).

Therefore, allusion – as well as the aposiopesis or reticence – establishes a sort of complicity between the speaker and the listener, between the writer and the reader, in order to reveal the "unsaid". However, what is left implicit undoubtedly increases the communicative force of the discourse.

The **aposiopesis** (from Greek 'I keep silent') consists instead in the sudden interruption of a message with the suppression of a part or in the direct allusion to something that is silent. For example: "He was a guy who calls himself quiet, but..." (graphically, the figure is precisely rendered using suspension points). Through self-censorship, reticence highlights the value of the "unsaid", and what is implicit comes to possess a greater informative content and semantic value than what is said explicitly. For this reason, we speak of "rhetoric of silence".

Reticence relies heavily on the interpretation of the recipient, who is expected to play a more or less active role depending on the discreetness of the modality used. This can also consist of prosodic means (suspenseful intonation for oral texts and suspension dots for written ones) and kinetic signals (gaze and averted gaze, facial expressions, etc.). The allusive power of silence makes reticence an extremely effective instrument of insinuation, suspicion and threat.

The **preterition,** finally, is a figure originally used as a remedy to possible violations of the criteria of brevity and adequacy of the speech, imposing to "pass over" (which is precisely the meaning of the Latin term). However, this figure represented a formal safe conduct and allowed to say the unspeakable, that is what could not be enunciated because rough or because marginal compared to the main argument of the speech. Even today, it is used to pass over something in silence at the very moment in which it is mentioned, thus emphasizing it. The use of preterition is easy to spot, since it's usually introduced by "I needn't mention …" or "to say nothing of …" or "needless to say …" or "it's not my intention to …" and so on.

This figure has an informative content of a metacommunicative type: it raises attention and commands the audience to reason about the unsaid. It is the emphasis of the unspoken, because it consists in saying that we don't know or don't want to say what we are saying most effectively at that very moment. However, this figure (like irony and other rhetorical figures) only works if the speaker and the listener share the same knowledge around the omitted information. If there is not such shared knowledge, this figure would not work or could represent an even more harmful (especially in a particularly technical and formal context) inference (which, let's remember, corresponds to a deductive judgment that results in an arbitrary hypothesis – conjecture or supposition).

To ask

The act of asking, in a discourse, can have very different forms and values.

A rhetorical question is a question that has no other answer than the (obvious) confirmation of what is being questioned. Thus, it is not a request for information, and it requires a response: yes or no. For example, "And isn't all this extremely boring?" [Of course, it is!]. The classic example of a rhetorical question is undoubtedly represented by the beginning (*exordium*) of the first of Cicero's four Catilinarians (these are four orations delivered in the Senate in 63 BC following the discovery and suppression of the conspiracy headed by Catiline). The configuration of the questions is such that it even reaches the tones of an invective:

> "How long, Catiline, will you abuse our patience?"

There is an insistent sequence of rhetorical questions, which end in the famous exclamation "*O tempora! O mores!*".

Questioning can nevertheless take the different forms of hesitation, conversation, and interrogation.

The pattern of the **hesitation** consists of the question addressed to oneself (e.g., "Am I making a mistake?"). It manifests uncertainty (simulated) between two or more possible interpretations, examining conflicting circumstances and opinions, weighing their pros and cons, with the aim to make a decision.

However, the speaker may need to insert dialogue parts within a discursive text, in order to give greater expressive evidence to the narrative. To achieve this, the **conversation** (or *sermocinatio*) can be used: it occurs when the speaker or writer reports a monologue or an intellectual reflection of their own or belonging to another person, containing questions addressed to themselves. Basically, one pretends to be asked questions and answers them. For example, "Some of you may ask me why I am addressing this topic in this way." This dialogic form can also present itself as the pretense of a question-and-answer dialogue between two or more people.

Instead, the **interrogation** (or *percontatio*) consists of asking questions to others (your opponent or the audience). For example, "Who among you has never feared for his or her safety in such a context? Of course, all of you!" The mock questions that the speaker asks, contain the opponent's remarks against which they immediately advance their objections, in the form of a response. For example, "-Telling him to his face made sense- But he didn't! -He thought he was there- But nobody saw him!".

Are words stronger than images?

We have seen how figurative language represents a tool of great ductility and power to express or even just reinforce words or concepts. However, how much can words compete with images?

Resorting to the 'visual' today is natural and practical. We live in an era in which images triumph, crushing purely verbal communication, in a sort of absorption and draining of words.

Even in ancient times, orators recognized the importance of the evocative power of images, but achieved it with words. According to Quintilian, the orator had to work to make their speech a "talking picture": they had to evoke virtual images in the minds of their listeners thanks to their rhetorical ability. Words were (and are) capable of evoking images. The *evidentia* represented that specific quality capable of giving to the speech the maximum persuasive force: it gave to the speech an effect of direct vision, describing the facts in the form of vivid mental images which were presented to the listeners with the same visual immediacy of reality.

For this reason, the *evidentia* was something more than simple clarity: because clarity concerned only the comprehensibility of the text, while evidence indicated a sensory fruition of it (therefore additional to clarity itself), so that facts were not simply exposed, but directly shown.

Thus, through the *evidentia*, the maximum persuasive power of the image was achieved: it was the image (of facts) painted in words.

Imagination (in Greek 'fantasy') is precisely the visualization mechanism of the verbal. It is precisely a mental mechanism of vivid representation by which one is able to directly see images of facts and scenes that they are not witnessing in person, with the impression of having them before their eyes. Thus, the text/speech springs that feeling of direct vision and expressive immediacy (which the rhetorical tradition identifies with the quality of *enargéia*).

Quintilian and his predecessors would therefore seem to have found a solution that preserves the word from the overwhelming power of images, leaving its communicative effectiveness unaltered: it is the word that becomes image itself. But can verbal communication today still manage to equal the persuasive power of images?

Images undoubtedly help to make messages more appealing, to make them easier to understand, and they are particularly useful in an age of scarce attention to listening, where it is necessary to fight boredom and deal with impulses that are very different from textual ones.

Visual arguments deliver a message in a multimodal way, which is then the way we have become accustomed to receiving and processing information today in recent years.

However, in some contexts (e.g., judicial, political, advertising), the prevarication of the 'visual' to the detriment of the verbal can hide many pitfalls. In fact, visual reasoning is not only fallible, but is also based on an abstract set of rules that do not follow the rational principles of logic. When we visualize visual information, we are rather susceptible to making judgments too quickly, unconsciously or based on automatic emotional processes.

Also, when we see something persuasive, we don't tend to ask questions about the underlying logic: we simply tend to believe that what we see is true and correct.

We can therefore agree on the possibilities of the

visual, but its use should always presuppose the enhancement and use of rhetorical thought, which can generate a 'visual' argumentatively founded, accompanied by the word that itself becomes image (according to the teaching of ancient rhetoricians).

Otherwise, we will only have a fruitless triumph of images without words, like beauty without intellect; and with the concrete risk of being dramatically trapped by it.

DECEIVE WITH WORDS

The "black" rhetoric: the argumentative fallacies

We have seen how logical reasoning, as a rule, represents the basis of any manifestation of thought, whether political, philosophical or even simply every day and informal. Often, however, such reasoning is flawed by some "logical errors of procedure" that are called "argumentative or logical fallacies", sometimes intentional and used as rhetorical devices, others unconscious and the result of prejudice or naivety.

The fallacy is therefore that tool that can make a speech poor or weak in terms of arguments, but persuasive. This is because – and it is worth taking up a concept already explained – a persuasive argumentation can convince even if it breaks the laws of logic. Persuasiveness is therefore very dangerous and, often, makes fallacious reasoning pass for good. In other words: it makes even a deceit appear sensible.

In the reasoning the fallacy produces the same effect as a false visual perception: it seems to work but, if you analyze it better, it hides a reasoning that is only apparently correct. On the other hand, in a false visual perception (or also 'optical illusion') we are led to recognize figures that do not exist or differ in particular characteristics, usually not visible until after careful observation. This happens because the human brain is attracted by some elements that are more common and known to it, or because it is deceived or disturbed in identifying the true nature of an image from the details. These phenomena are called optical illusions and are designed to capture the attention of the observer.

Similarly, but in the verbal field, the fallacies stimulate logically correct reasoning which, on closer inspection, does not work. Fallacies are wrong ways of reasoning because they start from false premises, or they adopt incorrect inferences, or they produce, in support of their thesis, irrelevant arguments from a rational point of view. Therefore, it is necessary to be careful in distinguishing the enthymeme from the fallacy: when in an enthymeme the premises are false, only then we speak of a fallacy. The enthymeme does not represent a 'fallacy', but we speak of fallacy only when the omitted premise is false. The enthymeme (unlike the fallacy) does not deal with imperfection but with the implicit, in order to become faster, pleasant, allusive, curious.

However, fallacies are widely used: one does not always want to appeal to the rationality of the interlocutor, and sometimes it is easier to focus on emotions or it is more effective to resort to deception. Because the fallacy is an error in reasoning that appears "psychologically persuasive".

Fallacies are used in the most diverse contexts, precisely because of the difficulty of being recognized as such: their apparent correctness makes them particularly suitable to manipulate the audience intentionally and fraudulently, in order to produce a misleading persuasion (e.g., many fake news). Therefore, we are dealing with logical errors that arise from the flaws (often intentional) of the arguments of many public discourses: from social to politics, from advertising to morality, from news to the various forms of storytelling. Indeed, it can be said that a large part of modern communication is affected by these 'flaws', including judicial communication.

Thus, in the term 'fallacy' there seems to reside in an almost natural way a negative meaning, because in fact fallacies are particular 'errors' of reasoning and are considered 'hidden persuaders'.

Let's try to understand how it works through an example, typical of a common interrogation technique. A question is asked that implies the existence of a fact or a presupposed truth: "After you killed him, where did you hide the body?". The questioner, whichever their answer is ('yes' or 'no'), inevitably admits the unexplained presupposition.

But the examples are countless: "Have you stopped beating your wife?"; "Have you had a lover for a long time?"; "Have you cheated on your wife more than once?"; "Why do you disagree with me?". In these cases – note – we are in the presence of an argumentative fallacy (the so-called complex question or *plurium interrogationum*) and not of a "rhetorical question", logically correct (we have already examined this in the previous chapter).

Numerous and particularly widespread, these errors in reasoning become dangerous 'hidden persuaders', even in the legal field, precisely because they concern the implicit and – through the exploitation of stereotypes – favor rapid decision-making mechanisms (which can indeed be 'falsified') and, therefore, the creation of real prejudices.

There are many different types of fallacies. The first classification is thanks to Aristotle who identified thirteen logical fallacies, distributed in two different categories: linguistic and non-linguistic fallacies. Since then, the evolution of different argumentative techniques as well as the evolution of language have left room for the constant creation of new argumentative fallacies. It can be safely argued that there are no universal criteria for classifying them. There are classification schemes that are very similar to each other in number and type of entries, but which classify the same argumentative scheme differently, or group argumentative schemes differently.

Let's look at some particularly used types of fallacies.

Fallacy of the false dilemma

It is also called the fallacy of false dichotomy: it asserts the existence of only two options from which to choose the true one, while there are additional alternatives. For example: "Either you are with me or against me"; "Either you go to university, or you will not succeed in life"; "Either you take to the streets in protest or you are at the service of the caste and the strong powers".

Appeal to ignorance

Closely related to the fallacy of the false dilemma, this is a form of argumentative fallacy used whenever it is inferred that a proposition is true simply because it has not been shown to be false, or that it is false because it has not been shown to be true. This is an obvious ploy, intended to reverse the burden of adequate argumentation. An *argumentum ad ignorantiam* basically has the following structure: 1) A is stated; 2) there is no evidence to deny A; 3) therefore A is true. For example: 1) God exists. 2) there is no evidence to show that God does not exist. 3) therefore God exists.

Fallacy of the irrelevant conclusion

This fallacy (also known as *ignoratio elenchi*) occurs instead when the reasoning formulated does not allow to prove the proposed thesis, but at most a different thesis. Basically, it occurs when one tries to present for good an argument in which the premises have nothing to do with the conclusion: it is a technique of escaping from an uncomfortable argument by presenting another argument off topic.

In Anglo-Saxon countries, when this logical fallacy is used in an intentional attempt to confuse or distract the interlocutor, it is usually called red herring. The expression derives from the custom of salting and smoking the herring (which with this treatment becomes reddish-brown) in order to preserve it for a long time. During hunting campaigns, smoked herring distracted the dogs from the trail and could be used by hunters to divert the dogs of competing hunters onto false trails. In literature and the cinematic arts, the 'red herring' is a narrative tactic aimed at directing the reader/viewer to a wrong conclusion (Alfred Hitchcock's use of it is exemplary).

Fallacy of the dummy

The fallacy of the dummy or puppet (or even straw man) allows to elaborate an unfaithful representation of the opponent, built in order to knock them down. The dummy is an excessive and caricatured reworking of the opposing thesis, in order to facilitate its refutation. The realization of the "dummy" is achieved by plausibly taking to the extreme the thesis of the adversary and then demolishing it. The fallacy of the dummy does not address the argument in question, it is a kind of *ignoratio elenchi*. Its function is to rise, based on the ease with which it can be demolished, a feeling of derision or disapproval that can be addressed to the real figure of which it is a representation.

Appeal to the people

With this argumentative fallacy (also called *argumentum ad populum*) one argues to justify a certain conclusion of one's reasoning by appealing to widely shared opinions or popular sentiment. But the positive (or negative) emotional value of an event, object or person does not imply a similar truth value (positive or negative: i.e., true or false) for the statements that refer to it. Political propaganda and advertising often resort to this argument, which take advantage of people's known propensity to accept anything that perfectly matches their expectations and beliefs (e.g., "How long will we have to tolerate our lands being invaded by foreigners?").

This fallacy is frequently used to feed and consequently exploit the sense of belonging to a community (e.g., the purchases of a certain brand or the participation in certain social media or even the assumption of stereotypical behavior).

Fallacy of circular reasoning

This is an argumentative fallacy (also called *petìtio princìpii*) that occurs when the conclusion is taken as a premise. More analytically, it is a circular reasoning in which something, established in the conclusion, is anticipated. The fallacy lies in the fact that the conclusion is already contained (often implicitly) in the premises, which instead should prove it. The classic theoretical example is amusing: a bank asks John to name a person who will vouch for him; John names his friend Anthony and when asked "How do we know he is a reliable person?", John replies: "He is: I assure you".

Despite its obvious groundlessness, this type of argument can still be persuasive if the recipient does not notice the logical error they have in front of them, affecting their independence of judgment.

The raven paradox

This is a fallacy immediately deriving from that of the circular argument, also known as the *Corax* argument.

The term *corax* ('raven') derives from the name of the Greek rhetorician (of Syracuse) Corace, to who – so it is said – the student Tisia, once finished his apprenticeship in rhetoric, refused to pay the agreed fee. Tisia wanted to provoke the teacher by explaining that only if he could persuade the latter not to accept the fee due would be evident that Corace had fulfilled his duty by teaching Tisia the art of persuading with words. Corace replied that if Tisia had persuaded him not to receive the fee, he would have deserved it, but if Tisia had not succeeded, Tisia would have had to pay: in fact, it could have been an expedient devised by the student to avoid paying the debt.

Beyond the probably fictional narrative (Tisia himself was nicknamed 'the raven', and it is believed that 'Corax' is actually just a fictional name to identify Tisia himself), *corax* indicates an expedient-reality dissociation used in conjectures. It consists, specifically, in doubting an argument because it is too strong, too 'proven'. It is a rhetorical device that serves, as Aristotle argues in the *Rhetoric*, "to make the weakest argument stronger."

> "if a given subject does not fit a charge of violence, say because he is of a weak constitution, the defense will argue that this is not likely; but if, on the other hand, he fits the charge because he is strong, the defense will argue that his guilt is not likely, precisely because it is likely that he is believed to be guilty" (Aristotle, *Rhetoric*, II, 23, 1402 a).

The undoubtedly suggestive strength of this kind of argumentation derives substantially from the fact that, at times, a truth that is too simple and obvious can raise mistrust by seeming too perfect to be true, almost 'pre-packaged'. Think about the legal field and the arguments that, too frequently, are built based on an obvious logical flaw based on the use of the argument *corax* (for example: "if the knife found in the house of the suspect was the murder weapon would not have been kept by the murderer").

Basically, as suggestive as the *corax* argument is, it is fallacious by being overcome with its own weapons, i.e., momentarily taking the *corax* as true, and then overturning it. The analogy is with the behavior of the raven, which, according to an ancient belief, when it is no longer able to provide its young with food, it offers itself.

Fallacy of well poisoning

The name of this fallacy derives from the ancient practice of poisoning one's own wells to block the invasions of enemy armies and is taken as an emblematic example of a technique as simple to use as it is devastating. It is a form of circumstantial *ad hominem* fallacy and consists of a pre-emptive attack that wants to undermine credibility in advance on everything, according to the following argumentative scheme: 1) A is unreliable; 2) everything that A claims is false or otherwise unacceptable.

Fallacy of causal correlation

Its classical name in Latin (*post hoc ergo propter hoc*) means 'after this, therefore because of this'. The fallacy consists in fact in sustaining the existence of a causal link between two events among which there is only a mere temporal succession. The fact that an event immediately follows another event does not mean that the latter is the cause of the former: the mere succession is certainly not a guarantee of the existence of a causal link. However, it is shown that our conviction of the existence of an objective causal link depends on the repetition of an experience in which 'cause' and 'effect' are regularly associated.

From these fallacies usually arise superstitions or conspiracy theories: for example, since centuries ago, immediately after the passage of a comet, a plague broke out, then it is deduced that all comets bring disasters and bad luck.

Fallacy of false precision

This fallacy is achieved when extremely precise numbers are provided, with the intent of inducing the audience to believe that the information or determinations presented have a special reliability. The numbers are used to make the audience believe that the content of one's statement is perfectly reliable, derived from official sources. The fallacy of false precision never fails to elicit an explanatory and self-referential evidence, often exempting the speaker enlightening data and numbers, as if they were immediately clear and persuasive.

Fallacy of hasty generalization

It is an argumentative fallacy, also called hasty generalization (or *secundum quid*). It consists in deriving a general rule from inadequate evidence, either because it relates to a special case, or because the sample considered is not representative. For example: "Since the assumption of narcotics is allowed to the seriously ill, it should be allowed to anyone". This trivial fallacy is frequently used (voluntary or involuntary) in newspaper headlines:

> "Warming up the planet? Although it's cold! – Snow in the mountains. And in Milan minimums at 5 degrees."
>
> (*Libero*, May 6, 2019)

The fallacy is evident, regardless of whether one believes in the global warming theory or not: in fact, logically, the journalist claims to derive a scientific rule from a merely occasional fact. However, they make believe that instead there is a scientific correlation, 'deceiving' the reader.

Statistical fallacies

The main characteristic of statistical fallacies, which they all have in common, is to infer, based on a few statistical data or uncertain data of unknown origin, unconditional conclusions that have the purpose of conditioning the audience (depending on the role, even public opinion). For example, imagine someone quoting an alleged statistic according to which 79.9% of summer fires are started intentionally. However, they fail to report where the observations were made, who the author was, and what methods of investigation were used. However, in the meantime, showing the data (often combined with tables and graphs) makes creditworthy the opinion of the speaker, giving presumed scientific proof to all that they summarily illustrate.

Another case is that of citing a statistic that is objectively true (a percentile increase, for example) but limited in proportion (0.001%) as an absolute positive value (an "increase", a "success", etc.), again omitting further references that would reduce its scope and usability and yet in the meantime generate a persuasive effect.

Fallacy of complex questions

It is an argumentative device that involves asking a question in a way that assumes the truth of a conclusion. For example, "Do you continue to use drugs?" The answer with a 'yes' or 'no' is reductive, since the question is precisely 'complex', and also presupposes (at least) another question. The aim is usually to catch the interlocutor unprepared, often concerning particularly delicate contexts from a psychological point of view. For example, it is also used as a common interrogation technique: a question is asked that implies the existence of a fact or a presupposed truth: "After you killed him, where did you hide the body?". The questioner, whichever their answer is ('yes' or 'no'), inevitably admits the unspoken assumption. But the examples are countless: "Have you stopped beating your wife? Am I the cause of your bad mood?"; "Have you had a lover for a long time?"; "Have you cheated on your wife more than once?"; "Why do you disagree with me?".

EDITORIAL STYLE OF WRITTEN SPEECH

Crossed words

The term (editorial) 'style' refers to all the features of a professionally written text.

The style also affects the readability of the text and, consequently, the effective involvement of the recipient (reader); lastly, it indirectly favors the acceptance of reflections and theses.

Clarity of ideas results in clarity of language. In addition to this, the ways in which a text is graphically written are also very important aspects. A graphically incorrect use of capitals, bold, italics, commas, brackets, spaces and so on will not help the understanding of the text, risking to damage the communicative relationship and not enhance the message presented.

The recent, progressive abandonment of paper in communications of all kinds has even amplified the need to convey harmony, even graphically, to the reader. This is because reading on a screen becomes unstructured: interruptions and jumps take the place of continuity and concentration, reading time is fragmented into many small parts, and the idea of a continuous text dissolves: a text is started and stopped continuously, even more so if it is on a screen, with the risk of forgetting what one is reading. Indeed, one should consider the fact that, unless one uses an eBook reader, reading on a screen is much more difficult, and is estimated to be 25% slower than reading on paper.

The objective of the written text becomes therefore that of accompanying the reader with pleasantness and effectiveness towards the full comprehension of what is being told and proposed, through a precise and luminous path along which they are never allowed to get tired or lost.

The font

A *font* is a set of typefaces characterized and united by a certain graphic style. According to the Italian *Accademia della Crusca*, the 'character' would actually be the single letter or number, while the *font* itself should indicate a composition of characters of a particular spelling (e.g., *Times New Roman*), style (bold, italic) and size. Today, however, in common usage the words *font* and 'character' are considered equivalent.

Key factors in using a *font* are readability and clarity.

The fonts most used today in typesetting are the result of centuries of research, both empirical and experimental, and have undoubtedly reached a high level of graphic and perceptive quality. They are commonly classified into two large families: *serif* and *sans-serif* (with tails and without tails).

Serif fonts are characterized by decorative strokes (tails, or *serif*) that extends off the end of a letterform, while *sans-serif*, or sticks, have no decorative strokes. The choice between using a *font* belonging to one or the other family of characters is not easy.

The most popular *serif* fonts are *Times New Roman* and *Georgia*, while the most popular *sans serif* fonts are *Verdana* and *Arial*.

It is generally believed that *sans-serif* fonts are more readable individually or in sentences of a few words, while *serif* fonts are more readable for long texts. The decorative strokes, in fact, help determine the shape of the letter and make it easier to read long texts.

But that's not the case for everyone. Some visually impaired people can read *sans serif* text more easily. People with normal vision do not find significant differences between *serif* and *sans-serif*, although most people prefer *serif* for long texts.

The choice of font depends both on physiological factors (the reader's visual acuity and the eye's ability to grasp them) and on cultural and environmental factors (the habit of this or that sign, taste, social habits). Also very relevant is the context (reading mode, in particular) and where the text will be written.

The focus on *fonts* is, after all, growing. The 2019 Paris Book Fair had the *EasyReading* font among its protagonists. It ended up in the spotlight because of its essential design: it is a hybrid font because it simultaneously presents letters with tails (*serif*) and letters without tails (*sans-serif*). This typeface was created by designer Federico Alfonsetti and immediately proved to be an essential tool to help those with dyslexia to read with less difficulty and faster. However, in general, this *font* increases readability for any subject.

Apart from specific *fonts* like the one presented here, for texts to be read on a screen it is certainly preferable to use *sans serif* fonts which are more readable especially when the font size is small compared to the reader's visual acuity. In fact, it should be remembered that the resolution of characters on a screen is lower than on paper: the low resolution does not allow the characters to shrink without losing sharpness because the *pixels* are not sufficient to clearly define the details of the letters (especially the tails, which appear so blurred).

It should also be remembered that the light emission of the screen makes reading more tiring than reading on paper. It is precisely to overcome the greater difficulty of reading on video that *sets* of typefaces have been developed that are more suitable to be used on a screen (and on the *web*), such as *Verdana* and *Tahoma*, both *sans serifs*.

In particular, *Verdana* (introduced in 1996) is considered among the most readable *fonts* on a screen, thanks to its well-proportioned and spaced characters, readable even with a very small body text.

In recent years, the *Georgia font* has also become popular. This font, an evolution of *Times New Roman* (1931), was created in 1993 and it is used by those who want a font that is easy to read without sacrificing the elegance.

Most people seem a bit distant and disinterested in communication in general, even more so in some (minimally) technical aspects of graphics. And yet, everyone should necessarily be confronted with this reality for the reasons briefly stated above. Therefore, we should not consider only *Times New Roman*, *Arial*, *Helvetica* (Windows) or *Calibri* (Microsoft), just because they are provided by the system or by the word processing software. We should consider if – given the change in context (reading of messages and documents mainly on a screen) – a more valid choice can be made.

Typographic printing privileges fonts such as *Garamond* (invented in the 16th century and today used by most Italian publishers in the *Simoncini Garamond* version, designed by a typographer from Bologna in 1958), *Palatino* (1948, used, for example, by Mondadori's Italian and foreign fiction) and *Baskerville* (1757 – used by Adelphi and Gallimard in France; in Anglo-Saxon publishing, Minion, Caslon, Janson and Bembo dating back to 1495, used by Penguin). However, for texts to be read mainly on a screen we can also use fonts with different characteristics such as *Bookerly (serif)*, *Caecilia*, *Futura*, *Georgia*, *Gandhi Serif*, *Lato*, *Libre Baskerville*, *EB Garamond*, *Source Serif Pro*, *Minion Pro*, *Noto Sans*, *Alegreya* (which make it easier to read long texts), *Fanwood* (ideal for increasing readability on portable media), *Crimson Text* (in the tradition of elegant old-style fonts but with improved readability on a screen).

Obviously, the choice of the font should be combined with the choice of the **size** (which varies, however, in the rendering from font to font – 12 points could still be an average valid size for most documents) and an adequate **line spacing** (1.5), able not to compress (partially obscuring the rods) any fonts with tails and allow a good level of readability.

On the other hand, fonts that are too small make it objectively difficult to read in any context; likewise, fonts that are too large (think of 15 and above) may appear not only inadequate for most contexts (professional, certainly, but also interpersonal) but even ridiculous (large sizes are preferred for direct communication, for example, with children).

Italic and round fonts

Any communication and document should show that its author knows how to use, without confusion, round and italic fonts (different from *Bold*). Italic should be used for:

- Latin or foreign language words or phrases;
- titles of essays, articles, and other contributions, as well as names of journals that contain them;
- technical terms;
- words or phrases to be emphasized;
- terms that highlight a meaning.

However, it should be remembered that a round font is more readable than an italic font: therefore, it is always advisable to limit the use of italic parts, preferring – for particularly long segments – the use of a round font between quotation marks,

Use and abuse of capital letters

The general rule to follow is to avoid emphatic forms of writing. Capitalization is one of them.

It should be noted, however, in everyday interpersonal communications and even in the most professional and technical documents, the invalid and unpleasant use of ALL CAPITALS (technically, **extended capitals**). The use of capital letters, today considered pandemic, was certainly born on the *web* and already some years ago. So much so that for *netiquette*, i.e., the set of rules of conduct aimed at fostering mutual respect among users on the web, writing in all capitals is equivalent to shouting. Yes, because whoever uses capital letters wants to be noticed, to impose themselves, to prevail, to prevaricate.

Some observers speak, with acute irony, of 'capitalism', indicating with this term the propensity, the impulse, the irrepressible need of those who use capital letters everywhere, almost always in vain.

It is not only a pure grammatical or graphic malpractice, but it betrays a real pattern of thought and behavior, in which capital letters are real doping to keep ideas going and a pathetic stratagem to stand out and be noticed.

Punctuation graphics

All graphic signs should generally always be placed right next to the word that precedes (such as the comma, period, semicolon, exclamation point, question mark) or follows (such as the opening parenthesis). Unbridgeable gaps such as those created by a lone comma are not allowed:

> "got into his car , drove about two kilometers."

or even by exclamation or question marks:

> "he wasn't even offered an alternative !"

Similarly, any double (or higher) spacing should be checked, preventing the creation of very large gaps (technically incorrect and visually annoying).

Harmony of choices

In addition to the choices that can be made, even in terms of graphic design and presentation of messages and documents, the modern speaker should still give absolute uniformity to the choices made.

So, there should not be a word in full and then later its abbreviation, or names and words not reported first in quoted italics and then only quoted or only in italics.

Just as clarity of ideas and clarity of language, the third link in the harmonic ideal of writing, represented precisely by the ways in which it is graphically transmitted, should also be dominated by balance and harmony of choice.

PARAVERBAL COMMUNICATION

Words are not enough

Verbal communication is the most obvious part of our communication: it refers to the use of words to convey, with conscious and effective use, any elaboration of thought.

The definition of verbal communication is therefore to be found in the language, that is, that form of communication built on the basis of a set of well-defined rules, aimed at transmitting information using symbolic mediators.

But this is not the only form of communication, because there are three levels of communication: verbal, paraverbal and non-verbal. Non-verbal communication includes all those aspects that go beyond the word, falling into the category of body language, while paraverbal communication refers to the way in which something is said (tone of voice, speed, timbre and volume).

Frequent statistical surveys show that in a communication the verbal content has a 'weight' of only 10%, the use of voice 30% and gestures 60%. In essence, voice and gestures would account for 90%.

Theater and its techniques have always had a significant influence on the formation of the orator, in particular on that part of the art of oratory that is called *actio* and that concerns the phase of declamation, or even recitation. This should not be surprising: rhetoric also concerns what is not exclusively verbal but accompanies, in fact, verbal language.

Speaking of the persuasive use of the voice, Quintilian argued that speech is more effective if the speaker is able to implement an "intentional control of emotions" whose manifestation in a more or less intense way occurs through a process of regulation. Also, in this case memory is indispensable, because it can determine how emotions are conveyed. Quintilian, in fact, recommends the memorization of songs that simulate the wide range of emotions, so that the control of the voice becomes an automatic factor. We are therefore talking about the concept of "emotional memory".

Not only stylistic models could be memorized, but also those related to the tone. In fact, those who improvise, says the author, are carried away by the state of mind and do not think about which is the correct tone to use; but if the student learns from the beginning to conjugate the voice inflection with the feeling they want to express, when they need to, they will be able to draw on an internalized patrimony of *pàthos* and automatically they will be able to implement the most appropriate *actio* or declamation. That is, they can adapt the oratorical performance to the contingent needs.

Cicero also moves on the same front, considering the theater a real model for the simulation of feelings through the voice: in fact, in a well-known passage of the *De oratore* (3, 214 ff.) he shows how the variety of tones of the voice is pursuable through art and reports a series of examples from the tragedy. The procedure is the same that will be later reported by Quintilian, that is the use of prototypes of emotions, memorized and assimilated and then reproposed in an unconscious and automatic way when needed.

This kind of improvisation, therefore, needs memory from which to draw on, like a reservoir, emotions and memories, which allow the speaker to appear really convinced of their thesis. Even if the speaker, while speaking, seems to identify with the feelings, it cannot be denied that they are the result of a careful process of planning and regulation aimed at the realization of a speech that is only apparently spontaneous.

Therefore, the art of improvisation seems to be reduced to a quality: the ability to adapt what has been learned and internalized to multiple circumstances. The ability to regulate and light up one's own emotions is, therefore, the result of a learning process and of a didactic strategy that does not totally reject spontaneity (as it happened in Aristotle) but makes the balance between identification and control its winning weapon.

By drawing onto the "reservoir of emotions", even the intonation of the voice will automatically adapt to the tone of the speech, contributing to its effectiveness, having previously assimilated the expressive correspondence.

The use of the voice was fundamental even two thousand years ago – Cicero (in *De oratore*) compared the vocal resources of the actor to the palette of the painter, who uses various colors to paint different people and to render nuances – and it is still fundamental today in any communicative context where it is necessary to involve the audience.

But what exactly is the voice, and what are its characteristics?

The voice: timbre

Timbre is the particular profile or distinctive character of a sound emitted by a voice. It is, therefore, the typical vocal register of the person, also called vocal color; basically, timbre is the element that allows us to distinguish one voice from the others.

We can describe a timbre with a multitude of adjectives such as enveloping, raucous, deep, lively, and so on.

However, depending on how we handle the other elements of paraverbal communication and on the communication needs, it is possible to give an even more pronounced character to the personal tone, or even to convey it differently with some environmental devices.

But not all the great orators of the past possessed vocal characteristics that, today, in a context of constant media exposure, are considered primary requirements. For example, reading Abraham Lincoln's speeches always produces an extraordinary effect, but his contemporaries testified that Lincoln had a rather high and thin timbre of voice, and that nineteenth-century audiences were not impressed by his manner of expression.

The voice: tone

Through the voice, fundamental paralinguistic signs are achieved to qualify the form of the verbal message: for example, the melodic variation of a sentence, the different intonations allow us to recognize if the sentence is interrogative, exclamatory, imperative, ironic, etc. But it is also a powerful indicator of moods and emotions.

Tone qualifies the communicative intention. It is an indicator of the communicative intention, of the sense one wants to give to what is being said: questioning tone, reflective tone, challenging tone, etc. But it also has a function similar to that of a highlighter when we read (for example, it allows us to emphasize certain concepts or verbal passages – think of the use of tone as a prosodic means of achieving emphasis). In addition, it can convey (and, therefore, let us glimpse) different moods (anger, serenity, joy, etc.).

The tone is also a very powerful element in making language take on one meaning rather than another, regardless of the actual verbal content. On the contrary, it is precisely the vehicle through which we can move away from the strictly literal meaning and achieve, for example, more complex rhetorical figures. For example, irony, where the message the speaker wants to transfer necessarily conflicts with the literal one, needs prosodic additives to promote full understanding. It is not uncommon, moreover, to run into attempts to create ironies that fail also because of the inability of the speaker to contrast the literal meaning with the right choices of tone and letting the attention of the audience remain on the literal content (in itself perhaps common, obvious, paradoxical or worse).

The voice: volume

The volume of the voice corresponds to the loudness of the sound and is used to emphasize concepts or reawaken attention.

Generally, people who use a low volume voice are perceived as shy, insecure and with low self-esteem. Conversely, people who speak loudly can convey confidence and self-assurance to others. But be careful: an increase in volume that is not appropriate for the context, topic or audience can also convey arrogance or aggression.

An example of an orator able to use his voice (and in particular tone and volume) in an excellent way is unfortunately the dictator Adolf Hitler. After all, a voice of two and a half octaves like his, was meant for remarkable modulations of rhythm, tone and volume. Hitler took full advantage of these characteristics by combining them with a vocal and postural technique that he acquired to communicate even better.

The voice: rhythm, pauses, accents

Rhythm refers to the speed of communication, which very often indicates a particular state of mind. From the rhythm we can tell whether a person is agitated, nervous or completely relaxed. But it can also be a specific way of communicating, independently from the situation.

Generally, we tend to speak very quickly in highly embarrassing situations (e.g., in front of a large audience).

An accelerated pace can cause tension in the listener; conversely, a slow pace can convey calmness and tranquility (but also boredom).

In this context, the use of **pauses** is a further element to underline and reinforce the verbal content, for example by creating real rhetorical figures (like reticence for example).

More generally, it can be argued that phonetic-prosodic elements (i.e., related to the sound-modulation of the voice) – such as accent peaks, speed increase, vocalic lengthening, pause dosage – even more if accompanied by proxemic indices (e.g., specific gestures), can consciously manipulate the speech. In order to understand exactly the power of pauses, let's take a look at the following sentence:

> "I don't believe that you, yesterday, were in the office with him."

It is apparently a linear sentence, with essential content. Actually, in this case, writing has less potential than speaking. Instead, let's see what happens when we read the sentence and place the accent-attention, with prosodic elements (therefore with the dosage of pauses and so on), on different parts each time, and verify the different meanings transmitted:

> "<u>I</u> don't believe that you, yesterday, were in the office with him."
>
> [someone else may believe it, but certainly not me!].

> "I <u>don't</u> believe that you, yesterday, were in the office with him."
>
> [needless to insist, I am convinced that you were not in the office].

"I don't believe that you, yesterday, were in the office with him."

[I have some doubts, but I don't believe it].

"I don't believe that you, yesterday, were in the office with him."

[definitely not you, maybe somebody else].

"I don't believe that you, yesterday, were in the office with him."

[definitely not yesterday, maybe another day].

"I don't believe that you, yesterday, were in the office with him."

[definitely not in the office].

"I don't believe that you, yesterday, were in the office with him."

[definitely not with him].

Obviously, through prosodic elements we can provide 7 different messages to the interlocutor, thus dissolving the ambiguity of a sentence that, if only written, can appear flat but also difficult to interpret.

Ambiguity etymologically means 'to lead to one side and to the other' and, on a strictly linguistic level, is the possibility of a sentence to take on different meanings while remaining unchanged. It is distinguished in lexical or semantic ambiguity and structural ambiguity. Lexical or semantic ambiguity occurs when in a textual segment there is a word that can have more than one meaning (for example the word "park" which can mean both a public garden and the verb parking a car). Structural ambiguity, on the other hand, concerns the position of words or verbal segments that can generate ambiguity of meaning: a sentence is structurally ambiguous when the terms contained in it have a single meaning (as in the case of our sentence), but their arrangement allows for more than one interpretation (precisely, seven interpretations in our case).

We can speak in this case of **fallacies.** This time they are linguistic fallacies, which can therefore mislead the reader or listener.

The fallacy of accent is precisely a common form of structural ambiguity that occurs when, within the same argument, it is possible to place the accent (i.e., the importance) on several elements of the same sentence, with consequently different interpretations. The context, the punctuation (in the case of written speech) or the intonation (in the case of oral speech) will indicate which of them is relevant (or to leverage it).

NON-VERBAL COMMUNICATION

When the body speaks

For many years, scholars have focused on the study of verbal communication, leaving out the non-verbal aspect as a possible source of interaction between individuals. When the study shifted also to observe the non-verbal component, implicit non-verbal behavior was discovered, based in particular on the observation of emotions, attitudes and conflicts (conscious or unconscious).

Non-verbal communication is based in particular on factors that are often not conscious but which, if controlled, can be used by the speaker to improve their oratory performance or, if they are skilled in interpreting these signals in their interlocutor, to use them strategically and adapt their speech accordingly.

We speak, in general, of **body language** because the human body continuously expresses, unconsciously, thoughts, emotions, moods, feelings, experiences. And every human being looks at the body of others, including everything connected to the body (for example clothes or accessories), just to read those inner and personal traits. The body plays a decisive role in regulating our relationships and our communication, and the complexity of relationships is also linked to the great ability that our body has to communicate. In short: it is really impossible not to communicate.

Non-verbal communication (also called NVC) consists of innate aspects and others learned over time, changing from culture to culture. However, it can certainly be argued that the ability to recognize the expression of the six basic emotions (happiness, fear, anger, disgust, sadness surprise) is widespread across the globe with a low error rate.

This type of communication is an integral part of our communication system, because it deeply influences the way we read and understand others: it is through non-verbal communication that we attribute intentions to others, that we create trust, credibility, authority; and it is always non-verbal communication that allows us to increase our self-esteem and allows us to better understand ourselves and others.

People who cannot read the basic signals of non-verbal communication are considered to have emotional illiteracy or alexithymia, that is, literally lacking the ability to read emotions.

The importance and enhancement of non-verbal language, especially for an orator, was already the focus of attention of Cicero and Quintilian. Quintilian expressly argued that the speaker should accompany their speech with gestures, not like actors (who mimic individual words) but by representing only the meaning; in practice, not by direct depiction but by the transmission of meaning.

However, let's see below what the basic elements of nonverbal communication are today.

Space

The human being is an animal, as well as social, also territorial, in the sense that they are engaged in the definition and control of their own physical and psychic space, in relation to that of others. The human being delimits and organizes the space, even excluding others and setting precise distances that can change depending on the culture they belong to.

Proxemics is precisely the science of human space, which distinguishes four types of distances: intimate, personal, social and public. Intimate is that which exists between two bodies that touch in the sexual act, in an embrace, in physical contact and are close to each other up to 45 cm. Personal is a distance ranging from about 45 to 120 cm and corresponds to personal space. The social distance ranges from 1.2 m to 3.6 m approximately: this is the distance that is held in hierarchical relationships and in more formal or work situations where there is no contact. The public distance instead is the one above 3.6 m.

In their space, the individual also takes a certain orientation, calculated on the basis of the position of the subjects (frontal, oriented at 45°, sideways, backwards). Orientation also implies a certain relationship between people: closeness, distance, openness, closure, hostility, availability.

Posture

There is a very close correlation between the body and its inner, invisible dimension: the body is the physical expression of a psychic dimension, and vice versa.

Therefore, every movement and every position that the body takes are the expression of a relationship between the inner dimension and social conventions. The object of study of **kinesics** are precisely gestures and posture, movements of the body, face and eyes, facial expressions and gaze.

Posture refers to the overall position of the body. There are three main ones: standing, sitting and lying down.

For speakers in an upright position, body control (we will see later) obviously appears fundamental. However, with regard to types of postures, we cannot remain silent about the extraordinary nature of another dictator: Benito Mussolini. He studied his image and the gestures with which he accompanied his speeches with particular attention, always assuming an erect position, with his jaw stretched forward, chest out, legs apart, arms crossed in defiance or hands resting on his hips (to convey a strong sense of security and power). Also evident is the postural choice of former U.S. President Donald Trump with regard to the torso (always erect, with a straight back, in a "posture of strength") and the head (which turns when necessary with a very particular movement, accompanying certain verbal messages).

Face

Unlike other animal species, and even our primate predecessors, humans' face has developed as a powerful tool for interaction and communication. Because the face is directly connected to the brain (the facial nerve that controls facial expressions is directly connected to the hypothalamus and limbic system) this makes it difficult to lie.

Facial expressions therefore have an important emotional value as they represent the immediate and spontaneous rise of emotions: each emotion corresponds to a facial expression (for example, you can smile with happiness but also with embarrassment, anxiety, uncertainty, as well as you can cry with joy or sadness).

Unlike other facial muscles, however, the **mouth** can be used to intentionally express numerous expressions and articulations, abstractly even not in tune with what is perceived (e.g., a fake smile).

In essence, facial expressions – as a whole – are partly intentional and partly spontaneous and can often result in expressive incongruence (more or less perceptible), even with respect to contemporary verbal expression.

It should also be noted that, in addition to the six fundamental expressions, there are micro-expressions, i.e., expressions that appear on a person's face for a very short time (from 1⁄2 to 1/25 of a second): therefore, they are so quick that they are not noticed except by slowing down movements.

More generally, **gaze** is a powerful non-verbal signaling device. In the conversation/dialogue it has the function of synchronizing (i.e., avoiding overlapping and favoring the alternation of shifts), monitoring (control of the interaction) and signaling (manifestation of one's intentions).

Your gaze can emphasize what you are communicating or, if you are not speaking, it can act as a support or contrast to the statements of others, or empathetically seek agreement with the audience.

But the uncontrolled gaze can also signal anxiety, embarrassment, insincerity, fear, or even submission.

Certainly, eye contact is considered one of the main elements used to create an empathic connection with the audience and, consequently, to promote its involvement throughout the speech (so-called engagement).

In the study of the non-verbal communication and the face, a particularly studied speaker in recent years is certainly Vladimir Putin, President of the Russian Federation. His impassive face, which many commentators have called "poker face" and many also envy him for it, has been the subject of numerous studies on paraverbal language and communication in general. The trainer of Putin's skills was undoubtedly Allan Pease, an Australian authority on body language. They met in 1991, when Pease was invited to the Kremlin to hold a seminar for a number of promising politicians, including Putin, who at the time was a thirty-nine-year-old former KGB officer in charge of foreign investment promotion and international relations for the city of St. Petersburg.

The first thing Pease says he taught Putin was to abandon the aggressive gestures typical of Soviet-era politicians, characterized by the tendency to wave their arms and fists (the reference is also to the episode of his predecessor Kruscev who, at the United Nations on October 12, 1960, as a sign of obvious protest, took off his shoe and, beating it on the table, continued to speak vehemently).

Putin has also another "golden rule" that he applies with great success in face-to-face conversations with other world leaders: he tilts his head slightly to one side and nods to the person he's talking to. "Research has shown that three consecutive nods of the head compel the person you are listening to continue talking," Pease states. "Therefore, he or she understands that you are interested in the conversation."

Pease, however, points out a feature that the Russian leader has not given up over the years, namely his "Soviet face". It is, specifically, a facial expression typical of Russian people, indeed "a specialty of Mr. Putin: instead of smiling like European or American people, they keep their lips closed and frown, as if to say 'Hello, I am your friend, you can trust me'", as Pease says. Clearly, there is a cultural legacy behind this facial expression: it, in fact, allows people to hide their emotions, which was necessary in the past for survival in an "era where it could have been dangerous to show one's true emotions on the street."

But analysis of Putin's paraverbal language led another researcher, Brenda Connors, to talk about "risk aversion" and "extreme sensitivity to criticism."

Putin, in short, represents an interesting object of study and also of reference in terms of non-verbal communication. But Putin's cold and neutral gaze is easily contrasted with the far more 'participatory' gaze of former President Trump. However, Trump and all those who have preceded him and will follow him have in common (at least for the last 60 years) an element that has greatly affected the 'gaze' of speakers all over the world: the 'teleprompter'. Electronic, of course. Exactly that indispensable tool which, placed to the right and left of every American speaker, allows them to read their own speech projected on a thin transparent mirror. The speaker seems to look towards their audience, maintaining naturalness and speed, and above all not losing the thread and avoiding dangerous deviations (useful deviations are called digressions in rhetoric).

Whoever thought, and still thinks, that the world's great political leaders, managers and many other figures can recite a speech while looking at the crowd and showing extraordinary memory as well as naturalness, was and is wrong.

Since the 1960s, the teleprompter (once part paper and part human – because it has to be flicked through...) began to make the public speeches of American politicians fluid and natural (and then showmen, the media, and the rest of the world started to use it). Everyone used it and still uses it, with different experiences. Former U.S. President Obama – whose speeches have always been undoubtedly meaningful in terms of content – has had no few problems in continuing his speech in the event of a problem with his teleprompter; while Trump, undoubtedly more imaginative (perhaps sometimes lacking in content), has always hated it, although he has always had to come to terms with it (and giving up the famous "off-the-cuff" speeches that so entertained the audience).

In short, body language certainly appears to be a fundamental object of study and learning in modern and effective communication, but the supporting technology has recently altered the direct relationship with the public. The risk that comes with the use of new tools, even in contexts that are not necessarily political or institutional, is perhaps that of losing a little (if not a lot) of naturalness: the gaze that follows a teleprompter or a screen, or a simple phone placed *ad hoc* to allow the daily speaker (youtuber or anyone else) not to lose the thread of their speech, is profoundly different from that of the adequately prepared speaker who keeps the speech in front of them or (where capable) only the fundamental points to follow. It's a look that can appear lost, sometimes ridiculous, not to mention the tragicomic effect if the support for some sudden reason no longer assists them.

Gestures

Gestures very often represent, for contemporary speakers, more of a problem than an opportunity. This is because they do not know and appreciate its characteristics and focus exclusively on content (and not even with certain results).

In reality we do not know our own gestures, which are often capable of damaging even worthy speeches. Let's think of an incessant rocking of the body, or repeatedly waving the arms, or also the casual and aimless use of the hands. In general, therefore, it is the total lack of knowledge and control of one's own body (and also of the surrounding space) that represents the speaker's first real problem.

So, let's try to understand first of all what gestures consist of. We can distinguish gestures into:

- **emblematic:** when they replace the word;
- **descriptive:** these are those that accompany and illustrate the speech, making it more vivid;
- **of regulation** of the interlocutor's behavior: that is, we are talking about assent, dissent, permission to proceed with a polite nod of the head;
- **of adaptation:** these are gestures aimed at dominating one's moods or emotions. We are talking about all those gestures, mostly unconscious, aimed at seeking a 'commitment' of the hands and, in essence, a psychological comfort: playing with a necklace,

mustache, tie, earring etc. (not to mention also gestures of a seductive nature, not necessarily conscious).

The hands, in the context of a more controlled management of one's body, are a powerful communication tool. Through the hands we can establish various types of relationships and we can express real concepts: for example, through illustrative gestures we accompany the speech to make it more vivid and effective, and through symbolic gestures we can summarize entire sentences.

Hands touch, shake, threaten or hit – they are a formidable tool for contact and exploration.

Palms, above all, are a powerful vehicle: the upward palm is a gesture of openness if not surrender, indicating submission and not threat (evoking a request for handouts), while the downward palm denotes authority, dominance, if not even possible threat: which is instead unequivocally communicated by the pointed finger.

Unfortunately, once again, the example of the dictator Adolf Hitler is the most relevant one, also in relation to the use of the body and especially of the hands. The analysis of his numerous public speeches shows a certain neutrality of the body, without any uncontrolled gesticulation. Then, in the moments in which it is necessary to signal fundamental passages of speech, he moves only one arm and always makes extremely measured gestures (for example, he points with his index finger, twirls a closed fist and moves his arm as if to dictate time). It is in this way that the immobility used until a short time before is magically broken by a few thoughtful movements full of meaning.

Subsequently, there has been no lack of speakers capable of making good use of gestures, such as Bill

Clinton. There were numerous speeches in which he undoubtedly showed his ability to contain and use body movements (in particular, his hands), accompanying words with perfect rhythm and integrating them skillfully with his gaze towards the audience.

KNOWLEDGE OF EMOTIONS AND STRESS CONTROL

Fear of public speaking

Even before fearing what to say, many people fear having to "say" something in front of others. A fear that represents the second most widespread fear (preceded only by the fear of death) and that, often, turns into a real terror, jeopardizing (if not preventing) oratory performances with worthy contents.

Since ancient times, **glossophobia** affects about 75% of the world's population: Aristotle himself always stressed his fear of public speaking. But he was only the first in a long line of celebrities who, though frequent public speakers, have declared that they feel anxiety during their public speeches.

Fear of public speaking leads the speaker to increased levels of anxiety and agitation. Their fear manifests itself in symptoms that can be grouped into three main categories: physical, verbal and non-verbal. And so, the speaker is faced with a constant struggle with their body during their speech.

Physical and non-verbal symptoms are definitely the

most noticeable and include increased blood pressure and heart rates, increased respiratory rate and sweating, stiffening of the neck and upper back muscles, dry mouth, if not also trembling of the lower and upper body limbs.

With regard to verbal symptoms, there may also be a change in voice during speech and necessary vocalized pauses (with the purpose of seeking stability); but voice tremor may go so far as to cause such difficulty that words can no longer be articulated.

Moreover, it has been shown that emotions can be diagnosed directly from the voice: consequently, emotions clearly and differentially affect the vocalization mechanism. The human voice not only allows us to identify the emotions of the speaker but can also raise emotions in the listener: listeners would be able to correctly recognize the emotional state of the speaker even only from vocal signals, regardless of information about the situational context, or other expressive signals such as facial expressions, gestures, posture.

Generally, people do not have difficulty in carrying out a neutral type of speech, while performance decreases if the speech has a relevant emotional content (and this regardless of a possible state of anxiety due to glossophobia). This is due to the difficulty in modeling and characterizing emotions present in the speech.

Many people believe, however, that their anxiety in public speaking is a unique and exceptional experience, that is, that it does not affect others: something profoundly wrong, given how common it is. However, it is true that this type of anxiety also differs according to the personal characteristics of each individual.

Some scholars argue that there are four types of

communication anxiety: anxiety related to the person's characteristics, anxiety related to the context, anxiety related to an audience, and anxiety related to the situation. Specifically, there are some people who are more prone to communication anxiety than others; however, numerous studies have shown how this type of apprehension specifically related to the characteristics of the individual speaker, can be overcome through adequate preparation and practice.

There are also several factors that intensify this type of apprehension: for example, the relationship that is created between the speaker and the audience, or factors related to the particular context in which the speech takes place.

The prevalence of this type of anxiety is also attributed to the fact that humans live in a particularly competitive age, yet have not been accustomed, for thousands of years now, to having to fight for daily survival. This would make their response to fear disproportionate or 'asynchronous' with modern life: that is, the same stress responses used for survival for millions of years are applied to non-survival situations. In essence, humans turn out to disproportionately experience emotional states that are objectively not extraordinary (relative to their history), but subjectively devastating today.

Emotions

But what is emotion? Current models hypothesize that emotions are responses to external stimuli and/or internal mental representations that result in physiological and psychological changes through multiple responses throughout the system.

The neuroscientific perspective states that **emotions** are a set of changes in the body state induced by the brain, in response to the contents of thoughts related to a specific entity, or a particular event, in the individual's environment.

Emotions should then be distinguished from **feelings**, which correspond to the individual's experience of these internal changes, hence the private experience each individual has when experiencing an emotion. Emotions are publicly observable, short-lived and transient responses, whereas feelings tend to remain active for longer.

Emotions arise when something important is at stake, and they elicit a coordinated set of behavioral and experiential responses that influence how we respond to challenges and opportunities. However, emotional responses can also mislead us, particularly when simultaneously physical and social environments differ significantly from those contexts that have shaped our emotions over millennia. When our emotional responses appear to be mismatched to a given situation, we often seek to adjust them in order to better achieve our goals.

However, before we learn more about emotional regulation, let's try to understand the speaker's emotional state in those very moments of anxiety.

The anxious speaker

The emotional state of the speaker with glossophobia consists primarily of two components: a primary central nervous system reaction and an interpretation of physiological responses.

The physiological state also labeled as anxiety does not differ too much from the feeling of anger or excitement. What differs is the mental label the speaker identifies in the experience. For example, particularly skilled and effective speakers learn to channel their body's reactions, using the energy released by these physiological reactions to show enthusiasm and stage presence.

In order to fully understand this type of 'stage' fear, and therefore the anxiety and stress of the speaker, it is appropriate to know roughly how the human brain works. Humans share with all animals a part of the brain called the paleoencephalon, also known as the archaic or reptilian brain. Within the archaic brain are the animalistic mechanisms of attack and escape, which are the two typical reactions of the animal when it feels threatened. Then we have the neo encephalon (cerebral cortex – where cognitive processes occur) and the limbic system that, although part of the archaic brain, acts as a link between the two brains. The limbic system, also called the visceral brain, is the one that receives the first impulses that it transmits to the two brains and presides over rather important functions (attack and escape behaviors, mood, memorization).

We can then imagine the limbic system as an immense archive that contains the different experiences of every human being. Each life event, once recalled to mind, causes a different emotion, which can be neutral or indifferent, pleasant or negative. And the same event can obviously create different emotions in different people.

What happens when the event is new? If the event has never been experienced before, the limbic system associates it with "events at risk." This is why the event of public speaking, if never experienced before, generally creates tension.

Faced with the perception of risk, the limbic system sends a signal to the pituitary gland, which is the control unit of the hormonal system. In turn, the pituitary gland reacts by stimulating the production of a hormone that helps to cope with the event: adrenaline.

The excess of adrenaline produces a series of organic reactions such as: an increase in blood pressure, an increase in insulin to obtain a better supply of energy, a faster and deeper breathing, a greater ability to concentrate and enhancement of the senses (sight and hearing). These are a series of reactions that strengthen the body to face that event in the best psychophysical conditions. Adrenaline, in fact, predisposes the human being or the animal to face the risk situation. Therefore, that tension should be experienced as a positive event that can even improve individual performance.

However, when our emotional responses seem to be mismatched to a given situation, we still try to regulate them: this is called emotional regulation.

Managing the speaker's stress

The concept of emotional regulation refers to the processes by which we influence the emotions we feel, when we feel them, how we experience them, and how we express them. Emotional regulation can be defined as an individual's ability to regulate their emotions, both positive and negative, by dampening, intensifying, or maintaining them.

Emotional regulation involves changes in "emotional

dynamics", changes that occur through cognitive and behavioral processes that influence the intensity, duration and expression of emotions. No type of emotional regulation is adaptive, but its functionality is linked to the specific context, the goals that the subject wants to achieve and its ability to inhibit behavioral and emotional responses that are not appropriate to the context. For these reasons, the ability to adopt effective emotional regulation strategies is a fundamental aspect for the adaptation of the individual, for their subjective well-being and for their ability to function socially.

Thus, it is possible to define **emotional regulation** as a multidimensional construct and below are some of its characteristics:

a) Awareness, understanding, and acceptance of emotions;
b) Ability to implement goal-directed behaviors in response to both positive and negative emotions;
c) Flexible use of contextually appropriate strategies to modulate the intensity and duration of the emotional response, rather than suppressing the emotion completely;
d) Willingness to experience negative emotions.

There are numerous techniques used to lower anxiety levels before and during a speech. The main ones relate primarily to the mental and motivational state of the speaker. In order to placate the fear of the stage, it may first be essential for the speaker to spend a lot of time **preparing** for their speech: nothing is scarier than facing the unknown. In the preparation process, it is then essential to break down the barriers of one's own comfort zone: adrenaline should be used as an engine to establish a relationship with the audience, which in turn wants to be part of a relationship and a sharing of emotions and content with the speaker.

Familiarizing oneself with the context also becomes a crucial factor in lowering levels of communication anxiety: the speaker, therefore, should acquire as much knowledge as possible about their audience, what to say and how to say it, and where they will deliver their speech (environmental conditioning can, at times, be as dangerous as a hostile audience).

Another element to consider is **relaxation**: there are a series of steps and techniques, of theatrical origin, that the speaker can use to counteract stress levels in public speaking. One of the most important techniques concerns **breathing**; deep breathing helps to counteract the effects of excess adrenaline, regulate heartbeats and blood pressure; **vocal warming** is also important to counteract this type of communication anxiety.

There are also some **isometric exercises** aimed at relaxing specific muscle groups, such as the act of yawning, which helps to stretch the key muscle groups involved in the act of speaking.

MEMORIZATION AND EXERCISE

Memorizing a speech

What do Hannibal Lecter and the ancient Romans have in common? In *Hannibal* (1999), the third chapter of the saga by writer Thomas Harris, Dr. Hannibal Lecter is described in several paragraphs as he prepares to cross a complex "memory palace" in order to recover memories. In order to understand exactly what this is all about, we need to jump back several centuries.

Among the ancient Romans, particularly effective teaching methods were adopted for the forerunner of public speaking. They were essentially based on two principles: repetition and memorization, taught to the students and practiced with a strict regime. After all, in a school where the book was a rare and precious aid, memory was the only resource the teacher could resort to.

The advanced student used to try to recite in front of the master pieces assigned to them and learned by heart, but periodically they also performed in front of a small audience, usually consisting of parents, relatives and family friends. Finally, only the most talented used to take part in real competitions of declamation.

This practice was repeated incessantly, to the point that Juvenal uses the metaphor of the heated cabbage to express the condition of impatience generated by the repetitiveness of the performances of the students in front of the master. Moreover, the poet specifies, they took place on a regular basis, more or less every six days, so that the teachers, forced to listen to the same things, risked exhaustion and students, obsessed by the fear of failure, spent their nights sleepless or tormented by terrible nightmares.

In the educational field the usefulness of the memory was, however, undisputed, even if it was painfully practiced. And no less important was its importance in the field of oratory, especially forensics.

Cicero in *De oratore* traces the origin of mnemonics to the Greek poet Simonide of Ceo (VI-V century BC): he, invited to the banquet of Scopas, a notable personage of Thessaly, declaimed a composition commissioned by his guest. He was away for a few moments and, because of it, he was saved from the collapse of the ceiling of the room. All the guests died, but it was only thanks to Simonides that the relatives recognized their loved ones, disfigured by the tragedy, and gave them a decent burial: he, in fact, saved their memory from oblivion by using a mnemonic device, which since then became canonical. He reconstructed, thanks to visual memory, the succession of places occupied by the guests and identified the victims one by one, connecting places and people.

The art of memory was therefore born in antiquity as a technique for the orators to improve the ability to remember, making them able to recite long speeches by heart, with great confidence and precision.

Memory, as we have seen, was one of the five parts of rhetoric, along with *inventio*, *dispositio*, *elucutio* and *actio*. This is the basic procedure of classical mnemonics: first of all, it was necessary to visualize a series of places (*loci*), that is, an orderly succession of spaces within familiar contexts (for example, the rooms of a well-known building); then, the various contents (*memoria rerum*) or key words (*memoria verborum*) of the speech were translated into interior figures (*imagines*) capable of striking the imagination and the emotions, which were arranged in the already fixed series of places, according to the order of the contents or words. Once the speaker had imprinted the complex of places and images in their visual memory, at the moment of reciting the speech they would walk through their inner building and, looking at the images, they would remember the "things" or the memorized words, while the places would give them back their order.

As with any learning process, Quintilian (in the first century AD) is not content with natural gifts but intends to enhance them through exercise: resuming the canonical distinction between *memoria naturalis* and *memoria artificiosa*, he insists on the need to enhance and improve performance through constant application. But we should pay attention to a concept that is also fundamental today: what makes us truly eloquent is not only memorization and declamation, but also feeling and intelligence. This is demonstrated by the fact that even 'laymen', when they are moved, always find the right words to express themselves. Memory – Quintilian states – is also restored on the basis of an emotional incentive.

Therefore, in mnemonics – as theorized in Latin

treatises – mnestic potentialities are activated only if affectivity operates in synergy with the rational organization of memories. An emotional shock can, for example, be useful to revitalize a memory; repugnant, unbelievable, unusual images – argues the anonymous author of *Rhetorica ad Herennium* (the oldest treatise on rhetoric in Latin dating from around 90 BC) – remain long in the memory, as well as resurface to the mind especially the memories that have marked our childhood.

For this reason, experience is fundamental in the choice of *loci memoriae*: when we return to a place in the past, we recognize it because the memories of what we have done there, the people we have met there, the thoughts and emotions we have experienced resurface. In the construction of the imaginary building of the memory, it is therefore preferable to refer to personal experience that allows us to fix the memory by anchoring it to images and feelings already known and sedimented in our unconscious.

The choice of these agent images (*agentes imagines*), however, cannot be codified. In fact, neither the Anonymous author of *Rhetorica ad Herennium*, nor Cicero or Quintilian handed down a list of sample images, useful for memorization: they are necessarily subjective, depending on what strikes the imagination of the individual person and on the emotions that, similar with personal experiences, are risen by those figures that are linked to memories.

As part of rhetoric, the art of memory was widely applied in the Middle Ages, especially within religious preachers. Franciscans and Dominicans were among the major users of the techniques of artificial memory, bringing significant improvements to the classical mnemonics: in particular, the Franciscans perfected the use of effective images, rich in emotional suggestions, capable of striking the imagination of the listeners and therefore, in their immediacy, more readily rooted in their memory. On the other hand, the Dominicans were interested in supporting, also with these expedients, the spread of both the Gospel and the systematic vision of the world and of God elaborated by Thomas Aquinas, and for this reason they developed a version of the art of memory that favored the organizational aspects of the mnemonic material, therefore more attentive to the structuring of places.

It was during the Renaissance that the art of memory experienced an extraordinary success: as the perception of the world changed, so did knowledge and, consequently, so did the need for new methods to manage its outcomes. Among these were included the techniques for memory, which were considered powerful tools for the vital organization of the data of knowledge, to the point of becoming themselves a valuable "key" to penetrate the foundations of reality. As an unsurpassable organizational tool, the art of memory is in fact exalted in the successful *Phoenix* (Venice, 1491) by Pietro da Ravenna, which Giordano Bruno (another author who will deal with mnemonics in an extraordinary way) will remember as the first and most significant mnemotechnical reading of his youth.

Then, especially in the 16th century, technical manuals followed one another, illustrating all the rules for the correct formation of places and images: real systems of memory that offered readers visual architectures, almost paths or 'theaters' of memory, designed to preserve and organize, in the most effective way, a large quantity of mnemonic data.

The following centuries have certainly brought many revisions and some innovations in the field of mnemonics: from the phonetic conversion of Stanislaus Mink von Wennsshein (later popularized by Leibniz), to contemporary mnemonists. The readers will have the opportunity, if curious, to deepen and find what might interest them most.

Certainly, the principles of classical rhetoric still represent undisputed points of reference. However we should take with a pinch of salt the numerous "tips & tricks" that brims this area: the efficient speaker should not be a man from the Guinness Book of Records, knowing by heart pages and pages of a speech or a quote, in an almost supernatural if not inhuman way. Because this could appear excessive for any audience and be perceived as an excess, a negativity, and distance them from a real empathy (which is triggered in very different situations).

Rather, the contemporary speaker should be familiar with the text and show naturalness in conveying it orally. This presupposes familiarity with the genesis of the discourse (in the sense of knowing its origin, gestation and subsequent realization, even when not one's own) and with one's own and one's audience's emotions (which also weigh heavily on the performance, sometimes prejudicing even valuable mnemonic abilities).

In short, the speaker cannot live on mnemonics alone. Then, of course, it may be nice to have a speaker who does not use a teleprompter or other media, and uses a classic paper outline, or a speaker who can read by memorizing the line that comes immediately after and handing it to the audience in a gesture of reaching them. All of this can be worked on; but we should always remember that the 'thread' can also be lost. What the speaker can never afford, however, is to lose confidence in themselves and in what they are doing, which is the real 'plot'.

Testing a speech

Everything discussed so far can prove to be rather useless if there is no objective possibility to make an oratorical performance, if there is no opportunity to test our preparatory work, our technical skills and emotional resilience. Without any experience in the field, it is actually impossible to fully understand the mechanisms of today's public speaking.

In short: training, specific preparation and – the third irreplaceable element – experience. The latter – it is banal to say – cannot be acquired in any other way; but it is still possible to carry out a preparation that includes how to test our work and our preparation adequately.

In recent years, technology has also intervened to try to respond to this type of need. For example, with the use of immersive technologies and in particular virtual reality (VR) for public speaking, that is, to allow a speaker to practice and simulate their performance "safely".

Most early VR applications for public speaking offered static environments where the user was situated above a pixelated podium overlooking a small, virtually generated audience. Today, these apps offer much more detailed, realistic, and most importantly, customizable experiences. Users have the ability to select the type of speech they want to rehearse and adapt it to real environments such as meeting rooms or theater stages.

A few recent studies have also found that virtual reality has become an interesting alternative for the treatment of social phobias such as glossophobia.

Thus, fairly recent software (e.g., *Virtual Orator*) offers virtual speaking experiences, where users can choose from different audiences based on their training needs, with the goal of helping beginners and professionals improve their public speaking skills. Similar applications are also believed to be used by training companies and therapists who help clients overcome their public speaking phobias.

In particular, apps of this type are considered useful for overcoming the fear of public speaking by practicing with a virtual audience, while also allowing the user to be able to analyze their skills through objective feedback. The user can decide the place where their speech will take place, the size of the audience, and the behavior of the audience according to their needs: friendly, interested, with moments of distraction, and even completely bored or totally disinterested.

However, the interaction that is generated is still limited: today it is unthinkable to imagine that an app can simulate the human context of an oratory performance.

Perhaps one should fall back on suggestions coming directly from classical rhetoric (the 'exhibition' in front of family and friends) or, with a more modern look, on recording or videotaping one's own preparatory exercises (listening to oneself and/or seeing oneself is always valid, as long as one does it with an adequate critical spirit and not as a simple mode of self-satisfaction...), looking for the perfect isochrony between gesture, voice and thought.

It is however always important to remember that excessive or obsessive preparation can do as much harm as its total absence.

CONCLUSIONS

The stated goal of this course was to illustrate how different skills are needed in communication: linguistic, paralinguistic, kinesic, proxemic, performative, pragmatic, sociocultural, psychological, and rhetorical. To mention just the essentials.

The goal in a slightly longer time frame is not to create an actor who is good at reciting a speech, but a man with basic knowledge at least in rhetoric, psychology and non-verbal and paraverbal communication, who is able to adequately deal with any oratorical circumstance, without resorting to clichés and stereotypes that many seek in the eternal search for the "WOW effect". Because – I will never cease to emphasize this adequately – the difference between a speaker who always uses the same tips & tricks and a seriously multidisciplinary trained speaker is the same as that between a trained monkey and *homo sapiens.*

On the other hand, the study of fundamental elements in certain disciplines can lead to the formation of a speaker by also conveying their characteristics, without excluding and limiting their creativity.

Therefore, we did not want to offer a manual of extemporaneous "tricks and secrets" to which to become dangerously attached, but a path to illustrate concretely how a real speaker is formed and acts, exploiting also their own specificities and ending up appearing a competent, aware, natural speaker and able to adapt to any circumstance that may arise.

If you have been disappointed by the absence of tips & tricks, I warn you that I am about to disappoint you even further: because all that has been said about very different disciplines is not enough. In fact, it should be analyzed further, with the necessary in-depth studies by individual specialists, in the awareness, however, that the methodological approach can only be multidisciplinary.

Let's say, then, that I've only taken you by the hand and given you an introductory tour. If you'd like, the journey is still very long but – I assure you – beautiful.

BIBLIOGRAPHY

Literary Sources

Cicerone Marco Tullio, *Opere retoriche*, a cura di G. Norcio, UTET, Torino, 1976

Cornifici Rhetorica ad C. Herennium, a cura di G. Calboli, Pàtron, Bologna, 1969

Quintiliano Marco Fabio, *L'istituzione oratoria*, a cura di R. Faranda e P. Pecchiura, UTET, Torino, 1979

Vico G., *Institutiones oratoriae*, a cura di G. Crifò, Istituto Suor Orsola Benincasa, Napoli, 1989

Dictionaries

DELI – Dizionario etimologico della lingua italiana, a cura di M. Cortellazzo, P. Zolli, Zanichelli, Bologna, 1979-1988

Dizionario di linguistica, a cura di J. Dubois, L. Guespin, Ch. E J. B. Marcellesi, J. P. Mével, Zanichelli, Bologna, 1979

Dizionario di linguistica e di filologia, metrica, retorica, a cura di G. L. Beccaria, Einaudi, Torino, 2004

Dizionario di retorica. Con elementi di linguistica, fonetica, stilistica e narratologia per l'oratore quotidiano, a cura di G. Sposito, Intra, 2020

Dizionario di retorica e stilistica, UTET, Torino, 1995

GRADIT – Grande Dizionario Italiano dell'uso, a cura di T. De Mauro, UTET, Torino, 1999

Il Vocabolario Treccani, a cura di A. Duro, Treccani, Roma, 1997

Studies and contributions

AA.VV., *Punteggiatura*, a cura di A. Baricco, F. Tarocco, G. Vasta e D. Voltolini, BUR, Milano, 2001

AA.VV., *Storia e teoria dell'interpunzione*, Atti del Convegno internazionale di studi, Firenze 19-21 maggio 1988, a cura di E. Cresti, N. Maraschio, L. Toschi, Bulzoni, Roma, 1989

Arcangeli M., *La solitudine del punto esclamativo*, il Saggiatore, Milano, 2017

Barthes R., *La retorica antica*, Bompiani, Milano, 1972

Bedini S., *Racconto & storytelling. Attualità e forme del narrare*, Franco Cesati Editore, 2018

Benzi M., *Il problema logico delle fallacie*, in Mucciarelli G. – Celani G. (a cura di), *Quando il pensiero sbaglia. La fallacia tra psicologia e scienza*, UTET, Torino, 2002

Berardi F., *Dinamiche della performance oratoria: retorica, pantomima e danza*, in Calboli Montefusco L., Celentano M. S. (eds.) *Papers on Rhetoric* XII, Perugia, 2014, pp. 1 ss.

Berkun S., *Confessions of a Public Speaker*, O'Reilly Media, Sebastopol, 2011

Bernardo A., *Le fallacie argomentative nella formazione del giurista*, in *Cultura e diritti*, 2015, pp. 15 ss.

Bernardo N., *Transmedia 2.0: Brand, storytelling, entertainment*, Armando Editore, Roma, 2018

Bettini A. – Gavatorta F., *New personal storytelling. Idee e regole per la narrazione del sé*, FrancoAngeli, Milano, 2020

Bobbio N., *Il linguaggio del diritto*, Giuffrè, Milano, 1994

Borges J.L., *La biblioteca di Babele* (1935-1944), Einaudi, Torino, 1955

Brambilla L., *Comunicazione non verbale*, FAG, Milano, 2020

Bruno G., *Opere mnemotecniche*, a cura di M. Matteoli, R. Sturlese, N. Tirinnanzi, Adelphi, Milano, 2004

Calamandrei P., *Elogio dei giudici scritto da un avvocato*, Le Monnier, Firenze, 1954

Calvino I., *Per ora sommersi dall'antilingua*, in *Il Giorno*, 3 febbraio 1965

Calvino I., *Una pietra sopra. Discorsi di letteratura e società*, Einaudi, Torino, 1980

Campisi E., *Che cos'è la gestualità*, Carocci, Roma, 2018

Carofiglio G., *La regola dell'equilibrio*, Einaudi, Torino, 2014

Carofiglio G., *Con parole precise. Breviario di scrittura civile*, Laterza, Roma-Bari, 2015

Cattani A., *Discorsi ingannevoli. Argomenti per difendersi, attaccare, divertirsi*, GB, Padova, 1995

Cattani A. et al. (a cura di), *La svolta argomentativa. 50 anni dopo Perelman e Toulmin*, Loffredo, Napoli, 2009

Cattani A., De Conti M. (a cura di), *Didattica, dibattito, fallacie e altri campi dell'argomentazione*, Loffredo, Napoli, 2012

Cicchetti M., *Il corpo che parla: viaggio nel mondo della comunicazione non verbale per riconoscere i segnali del corpo*, Albatros, Roma, 2013

Citro A., *Emotional branding: lo storytelling nel marketing*, Santelli, 2020

Copi I. M., Cohen C., *Introduzione alla logica*, Il Mulino, Bologna, 1997

Corsaro M., *La Comunicazione non verbale. Analisi del linguaggio corporeo*, Aracne, Roma, 2011

Cuoghi A., Golfera G., Manocchi P., *Tecniche di lettura veloce e memorizzazione*, Il Sole 24 Ore, Milano, 2010

De Mauro T., *Capire le parole*, Laterza, Roma-Bari, 1994

De Mauro T., *Guida all'uso delle parole*, Editori Riuniti, Roma, 2003 (1980)

Di Nicola F., *Il marketing della paura. Donald Trump e il codice della comunicazione politica*, Castelvecchi, Roma, 2020

Eco U., *Semiotica e filosofia del linguaggio*, Einaudi, Torino, 1984

Eco U., *Il secondo diario minimo*, Bompiani, Milano, 1992

Eco U., *Mnemotecniche e rebus*, San Marino University Press, Guaraldi, Rimini, 2013

Ekman P., Friesen W.V., *Giù la maschera. Come riconoscere le emozioni dall'espressione del viso*, Giunti, Firenze, 2017

Ekman P., *I volti della menzogna. Gli indizi dell'inganno nei rapporti interpersonali, negli affari, nella politica, nei tribunali*, Giunti, Firenze, 2015

Ellero M.P., *Retorica. Guida all'argomentazione e alle figure del discorso*, Carocci, Roma, 2017

Fabiani P., *Il cerchio delle illusioni. Arte della memoria ed esperienza dell'immaginazione*, Libri Liberi, Firenze, 2010

Ferrari A., *Le ragioni del testo*, Accademia della Crusca, Firenze, 2003

Ferraro G., *Teorie della narrazione: dai racconti tradizionali all'odierno storytelling*, Carocci, Roma, 2020

Fioritto A. (a cura di), *Manuale di stile. Strumenti per semplificare il linguaggio delle amministrazioni pubbliche*, Dipartimento della funzione pubblica, Il Mulino, Bologna, 1997

Folena U., *Tutto maiuscolo, vizio di questa stagione*, in *Avvenire.it*, 24 novembre 2019

Fontana A., *Manuale di Storytelling. Raccontare con efficacia prodotti, marchi e identità di impresa*, Etas, 2009

Fontanier P., *Les figures du discours*, Flammarion, Paris, 1977 (1827)

Fumaroli M., *L'età dell'eloquenza*, Adelphi, Milano, 2002 (1980)

Gallo C., *Comunicare come Steve Jobs e i migliori oratori degli eventi TED. I segreti di un discorso vincente*, Vallardi, 2016

Garfield S., *Sei proprio il mio typo. La vita segreta dei caratteri tipografici*, TEA, Milano, 2015

Grice H.P., *Logica e conversazione*, il Mulino, Bologna, 1993 (1989)

Gruppo μ, *Retorica generale. Le figure della comunicazione*, Bompiani, Milano, 1976 (1970)

Jacobson R., *Saggi di linguistica generale*, Feltrinelli, Milano, 1983 (1963)

Jar N., *La comunicazione non verbale: il silenzioso linguaggio oltre le parole*, Hachette, Milano, 2018

Kennedy G., *The Art of Persuasion in Greece*, Princeton University Press, Princeton, 1970

Kennedy G., *The Art Thetoric in the Roman World*, Princeton University Press, Princeton, 1972

Kennedy G., *A New History of Classical Rhetoric*, Princeton University Press, Princeton, 1994

Khan F., Sarosh I., Shafique M., Kulsoom G., Ali A., *Glossophobia among Undergraduate Students of Government Medical Colleges in Karachi*, in *International Journal of Research* (IJR), 2015, pp. 110 ss.

Lausberg H., *Elementi di retorica*, il Mulino, Bologna, 1969 (1949)

Lesina R., *Il Nuovo Manuale di Stile*, Zanichelli, Bologna, 2009

Linklater. K., *La voce naturale. Immagini e pratiche per un uso efficace della voce e del linguaggio*, FrancoAngeli, Milano, 2019

Luccone L. G., Questione di virgole. Punteggiare rapido e accorto, Laterza, Roma-Bari, 2018

Lupton E., Brazzali M., Decarli R., *Caratteri, testo, gabbia.*

Guida critica alla progettazione grafica, Zanichelli, Bologna, 2010

Lurija A., *Viaggio nella mente di un uomo che non dimenticava nulla*, Armando, Roma, 1979 (1968)

Lurija A., *Un mondo perduto e ritrovato*, Editori Riuniti, Roma, 1979

Lurija A., *Neuropsicologia della memoria*, Editori Riuniti, Roma, 1981

Manenti L. G., *Frances A. Yates e l'arte della memoria fra classicità e Rinascimento*, in *Metabasis.it, Rivista Internazionale di Filosofia Online*, 2012, 14

Manzoni G., *Il linguaggio del corpo: tra oratore e attore*, in *Acme*, 2/2017, doi.org/10.13130/2282-0035/9359

Menchetelli V., *Archiviare, ricordare, obliare. Note sulle connessioni interdisciplinari tra memoria e rappresentazione*, FrancoAngeli, Milano, 2020, doi.org/10.3280/oa-548.133

Micheletti L., *Empatia e comunicazione non verbale*, Pellegrini, Cosenza, 2017

Mortara Garavelli B., *Le parole e la giustizia. Divagazioni grammaticali e retoriche su testi giuridici italiani*, Einaudi, Torino, 2001

Mortara Garavelli B., *Prontuario di punteggiatura*, Laterza, Roma-Bari, 2003

Mortara Garavelli B. (a cura di), *Storia della punteggiatura in Europa*, Laterza, Roma-Bari, 2008

Mortara Garavelli B., *Manuale di retorica*, Bompiani, Milano, 2019 (1988)

Nocchi F.R., *Giocolieri, prestigiatori e oratori: il ruolo delle emozioni nell'arte dell'improvvisazione*, in *Archivi delle emozioni*, 1, 2020, pp. 37 ss.

Orzati D., *Visual storytelling: quando il racconto si fa immagine*, Hoepli, Milano, 2019

Pease A. & B., *Perché mentiamo con gli occhi e ci vergogniamo con i piedi?*, BUR, Milano, 2008

Perelman C., Olbrechts-Tyteca L., *Trattato dell'argomentazione. La nuova retorica*, Einaudi, Torino, 2013 (1958)

Perissinotto A., *Raccontare. Strategie e tecniche di storytelling*, Laterza, Roma-Bari, 2020

Piattelli Palmarini M., *L'arte di persuadere. Come impararla, come esercitarla, come difendersene*, Mondadori, Milano, 1995

Plebe A., *Breve storia della retorica antica*, Laterza, Roma-Bari, 1988 (1961)

Plebe A., Emanuele P., *Manuale di retorica*, Laterza, Roma-Bari, 1988

Preti H., *Retorica e logica. Le due culture*, Einaudi, Torino, 1968

Raimondi E., *La retorica d'oggi*, il Mulino, Bologna, 2002

Reboul O., *Introduzione alla retorica*, il Mulino, Bologna, 1996 (1994)

Rigotti F., *La verità retorica. Etica, conoscenza, persuasione*, Feltrinelli, Milano, 1995

Rossi P., *Clavis universalis. Arti mnemoniche e logica combinatoria da Lullo a Leibniz*, Il Mulino, Bologna, 1983 (1960)

Rossi P., *Chi erano gli artisti della memoria?*, in *Comprendre, Archive International pour l'Anthropologie et la Psychopathologie Phénoménologiques*, 2008, pp. 312 ss.

Sachs O., *L'uomo che scambiò sua moglie per un cappello*, Adelphi, Milano, 1986 (1985)

Sagnotti S.C., *Retorica e logica. Aristotele, Cicerone, Quintiliano, Vico*, Giappichelli, Torino, 1999

Salvo M., *Il segreto di una memoria prodigiosa. Tecniche di memorizzazione rapida*, Mondadori, 2011

Schopenauer A., *L'arte di ottenere ragione esposta in 38 stratagemmi*, Adelphi, Milano, 1991 (1830)

Serianni L., *Grammatica italiana*, UTET, Torino, 1989

Serianni L., *Prima lezione di grammatica*, Laterza, Roma-Bari, 2006

Serianni L., *Italiani scritti*, il Mulino, Bologna, 2007

Serianni L., *Leggere, scrivere, argomentare. Prove ragionate di scrittura*, Laterza, Roma-Bari, 2013

Silverman L.L., *Wake Me Up When the Data Is Over: How Organizations Use Stories to Drive Results*, John Wiley & Sons, San Francisco, 2006

Sposito G., *Il luogo dell'oratore. Argomentazione topica e retorica forense in Cicerone*, ESI, Napoli, 2001

Sposito G., *In nome della lingua italiana. Manuale di scrittura forense*, Intra, Pesaro, 2020

Sposito G., *Manuale di retorica forense*, Intra, Pesaro, 2023

Sposito G., *Quanto siamo retorici. Libera l'oratore che è in te*, Intra, Pesaro, 2020

Sposito G., *Prima di giudicare. Stereotipi e pregiudizi in dieci grandi processi*, Intra, Pesaro, 2020

Storr W., La *scienza dello storytelling. Come le storie incantano il cervello*, Codice, Torino, 2020

Tallarita, A.L., *Il potere della voce. Per un uso consapevole dello strumento vocale*, Aracne, Canterano, 2019

Taruffo M., *Note sintetiche sulla sinteticità*, in *Rivista trimestrale di diritto e procedura civile*, 2017, pp. 452 ss.

Toulmin S., *Gli usi dell'argomentazione*, Rosenberg & Sellier, Torino, 1975 (1958)

Vickers B, *Storia della retorica*, il Mulino, Bologna, 1994 (1989)

Viennot B., La lingua di Trump, Einaudi, Torino, 2019

Visconti J., *La chiarezza tra superfluo e necessario*, in *Breviario per una buona scrittura*, Gruppo di lavoro sulla chiarezza e la sinteticità degli atti processuali, Ministero della Giustizia, Roma, 16 febbraio 2018, pp. 15 ss.

Woods J., Irvine A., Walton D., *Argument: critical Thinking. Logic and the Fallacies*, Prentice Hall, Toronto, 2000

Yates F., *L'arte della memoria*, Einaudi, Torino, 1993 (1966)

edizioni intra

SERIES

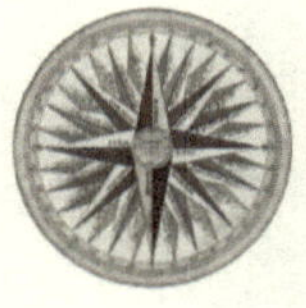

Il Disoriente
Great Classic Novels
Pirandello Short Stories for a Year
Thriller & Noir
Science-Fiction, Fantasy & Adventure

Mysteria
Mystery Stories & Essays

Astra
Stories and tales. Beyond the Earth

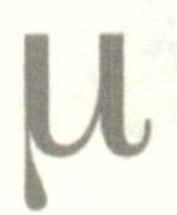

Saggiamente
Essays on human and social sciences

Retoricamente
Essays and handbooks on rhetoric, language and public speaking

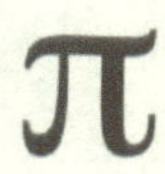

Politicamente
Political essays and writings

Brĕvitĕr
Legal handbooks

Visio
Graphic and visual arts

Teatro da leggere
Plays

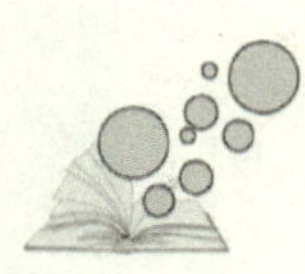

Mille bolle blu
Books for children

www.intrapublishing.com

www.ingramcontent.com/pod-product-compliance
Lightning Source LLC
LaVergne TN
LVHW091057150826
845673LV00002B/617